PUZZLES
for
WRINKLIES

This edition published in 2014 by Prion
An imprint of the Carlton Publishing Group
20 Mortimer Street
London W1T 3JW

A CIP catalogue for this book is available from the British Library.

ISBN 978 1 85375 774 7

Printed in the UK by CPI Group (UK) Ltd, Croydon, CR0 4YY

10 9 8 7 6 5 4 3

The puzzles in this book previously appeared in *Brain Training Puzzles: Quick Book 1*, *Brain Training Puzzles: Intermediate Book 1* and *Brain Training Puzzles: Hard Book 1*,

PUZZLES
~for~
WRINKLIES
Clever Conundrums for Older Intellects

PRION

CONTENTS

INTRODUCTION

Welcome to this jolly book of puzzles and quotes that has been speciallyy designed to entertain you, the happy-go-lucky, freedom-loving wrinkly. Now you already know that a big part of youth is stored in the brain. "You're as old as you feel", and all that. But it's also true that as one matures (yes, I mean you're getting a bit older) one needs to ensure sure that the brain gets regular exercise – just as with your body. Luckily for all of us, brain exercise can be done from the comfort of a favourite armchair. That's where this book comes in. Do a few puzzles a day and keep your grey matter in great shape! As well as the wide variety of puzzles inside, we've included some funny, uplifting and downright silly quotations for you too, so you won't get bored.

Enjoy the book, and keep yourself young!

EASY
PUZZLES

MASYU: Draw a single unbroken line around the grid that passes
through all the circles. The line must enter and leave each box in the centre of one
of its four sides.
Black Circle: Turn left or right in the box, and the line must pass straight through
the next and previous boxes.
White Circle: Travel straight through the box, and the line must turn in the next
and/or previous box.

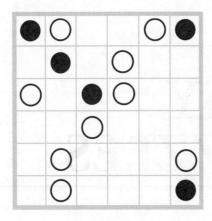

Answer on page 156

BITS AND PIECES: Can you match the four
halves of broken plate?

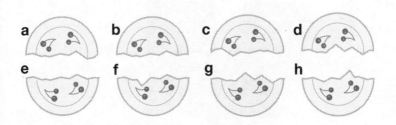

Answer on page 156

7

BOXES: Playing the game of boxes, each player takes it in turns to join two adjacent dots with a line. If a player's line completes a box, the player wins the box and has another go. It's your turn in the game below. To avoid giving your opponent a lot of boxes, what's your best move?

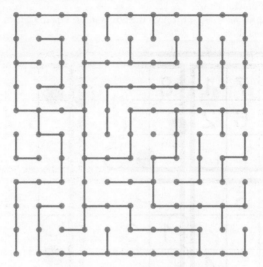

Answer on page 156

CAN YOU CUT IT?: Cut a straight line through this shape to create two shapes that are identical.

Answer on page 156

SUDOKU: Complete the grid so that the numbers 1, 2, 3, 4, 5, 6, 7, 8 and 9 appear once only in each row, column and 9x9 square.

	7	1	8		6			
	6	2						
5				1				
2	5							4
			1	3				7
		4						
	1				9			
		6				7		
9				4		3	5	

Answer on page 156

WHERE'S THE PAIR?: Only two of the shapes
below are exactly the same, can you find the matching pair?

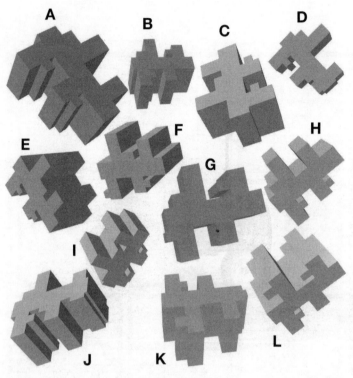

A B C D

E F H

G

I

J K L

Answer on page 156

RIDDLE: On this island in the middle of a lake, there is a tractor, used in summer to give tourists rides around the place. The tractor didn't get there by boat or by air, and it wasn't built there either... so how did it get there?

Answer on page 156

ODD CLOCKS: Buenos Aires is 13 hours behind
Melbourne, which is 9 hours ahead of London. It is 12.35 pm on Wednesday in
Melbourne – what time is it in the other two cities?

MELBOURNE

LONDON   **BUENOS AIRES**

Answer on page 156

SUM TOTAL: Replace the question marks with
mathematical symbols (+, –, × or ÷) to make a working sum.

Answer on page 158

CHECKERS:
Make a move for white so that eight black pieces are left, none of which are in the same column or row.

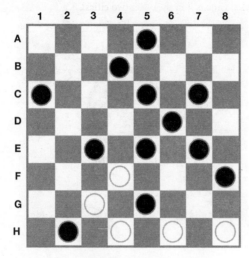

Answer on page 157

CUT AND FOLD:
Which of the Patterns below is created by this fold and cut?

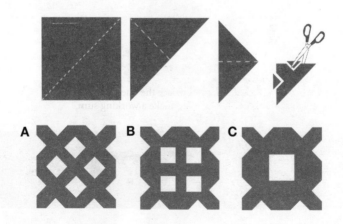

Answer on page 157

13

DOUBLE DRAT: All these shapes appear twice in the box except one. Can you spot the singleton?

Answer on page 157

GAME OF TWO HALVES: Which two shapes below will pair up to create the top shape?

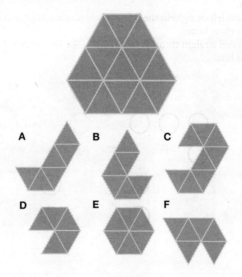

Answer on page 157

GRIDLOCK: Which square correctly completes the grid?

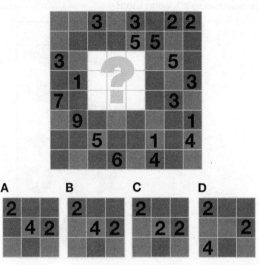

Answer on page 157

MASYU: Draw a single unbroken line around the grid that passes
through all the circles. The line must enter and leave each box in the centre of one
of its four sides.

Black Circle: Turn left or right in the box, and the line must pass straight through
the next and previous boxes.

White Circle: Travel straight through the box, and the line must turn in the next
and/or previous box.

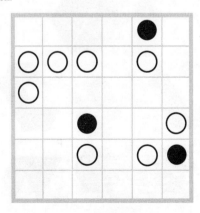

Answer on page 157

MINI NONOGRAM: The numbers by each row and column describe black squares and groups of black squares that are adjoining. Colour in all the black squares and a six number combination will be revealed.

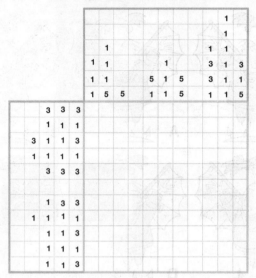

Answer on page 157

PICTURE PARTS: Which box contains exactly the right bits to make the pic?

Answer on page 157

MIRROR IMAGE: Only one of these pictures is an exact mirror image of the first one? Can you spot it?

Answer on page 157

WHERE'S THE PAIR?: Only two of these

pictures are exactly the same. Can you spot the matching pair?

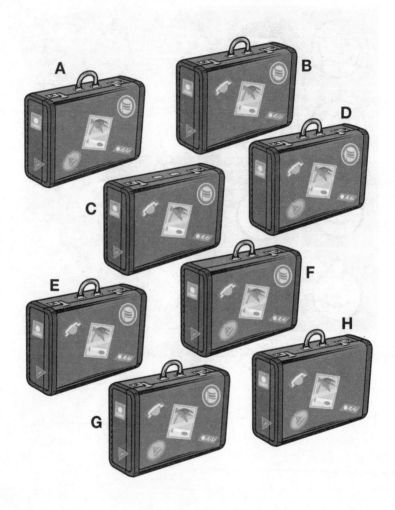

Answer on page 158

SUM PEOPLE: Work out what number is represented by which person and replace the question mark.

Answer on page 158

SUDOKU: Complete the grid so that the numbers 1, 2, 3, 4, 5, 6, 7, 8 and 9 appear once only in each row, column and 9x9 square.

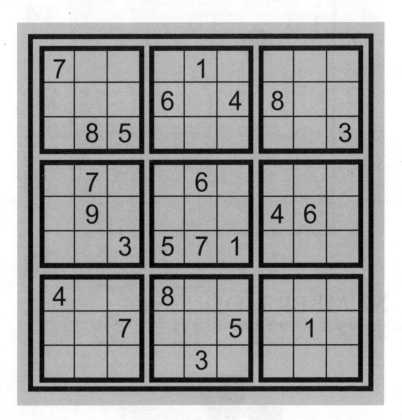

Answer on page 158

SHAPE SHIFTING: Fill in the empty squares so
that each row, column and long diagonal contains five different symbols

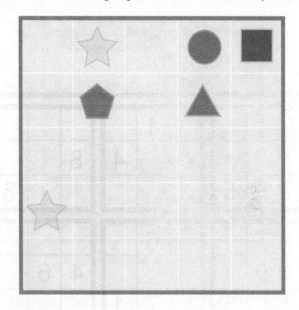

Answer on page 158

NUMBER MOUNTAIN: Replace the
question marks with numbers so that each pair of blocks adds up to the block
directly above them.

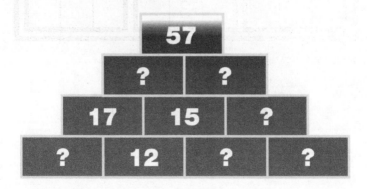

Answer on page 158

POTS OF DOTS: How many dots should there be in the hole in this pattern?

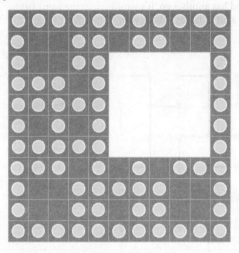

Answer on page 158

BLOCK PARTY: Assuming all blocks that are not visible from this angle are present, how many blocks have been removed from this 5 × 5 × 5 cube?

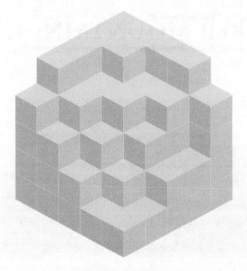

Answer on page 158

BOXES: Playing the game of boxes, each player takes it in turns to

join two adjacent dots with a line. If a player's line completes a box, the player wins the box and has another go. It's your turn in the game below. To avoid giving your opponent a lot of boxes, what's your best move?

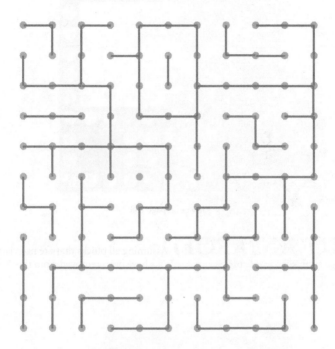

Answer on page 159

CATS AND COGS: Turn the handle in the indicated direction... Does the cat go up or down?

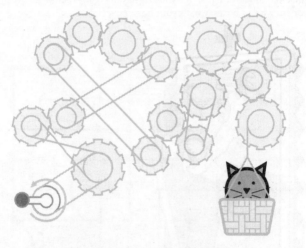

Answer on page 159

CUT AND FOLD: Which of the patterns below is created by this fold and cut?

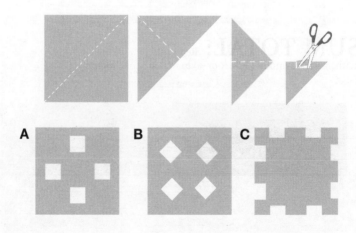

A   **B**   **C**

Answer on page 159

RIDDLE: When the new hospital was built, Big Dave was hired to paint the numbers 1 to 100 on the rooms. How many times will Dave be painting the number 9?

Answer on page 159

SUM TOTAL: Replace the question marks with mathematical symbols (+, −, × or ÷) to make a working sum.

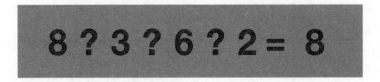

$$8 ? 3 ? 6 ? 2 = 8$$

Answer on page 159

ODD CLOCKS: Karachi is 4 hours ahead of Paris, which is 8 hours behind Tokyo. It is 9.05 pm on Thursday in Paris – what time is it in the other two cities?

PARIS

TOKYO   **KARACHI**

Answer on page 159

POTS OF DOTS: How many dots should there be in the hole in this pattern?

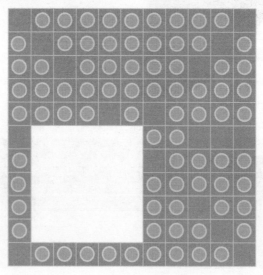

Answer on page 159

RIDDLE: At the auction house, George and Jenna were browsing through the items before the sale began. George had his eye on a ceremonial sword, inscribed to "Captain Beswick Alistair Campbell, for Exceptional Valour in the Field, Belgium, November 12th 1917, WWI". Jenna told him not to be daft, it was forgery! How did she know?

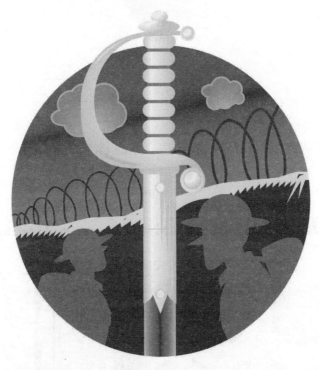

Answer on page 159

27

GAME OF TWO HALVES: Which two

shapes below will pair up to create the top shape?

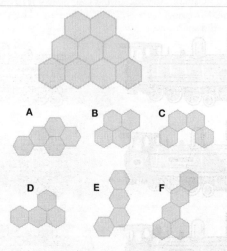

Answer on page 160

MATRIX: Which of the boxed figures completes the set?

Answer on page 160

WHERE'S THE PAIR?: Only two of these
pictures are exactly the same. Can you spot the matching pair?

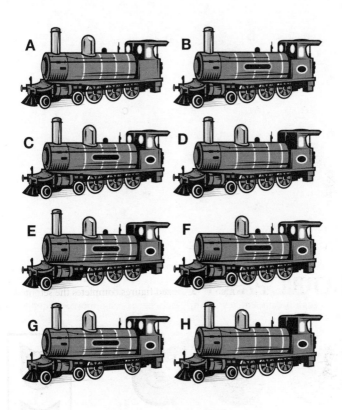

Answer on page 160

BITS AND PIECES: Can you match four pieces twice to make two letters of the alphabet?

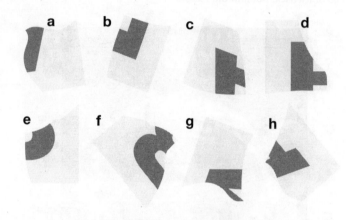

Answer on page 160

BLOCK PARTY: Assuming all blocks that are not visible from this angle are present, how many blocks have been removed from this 5 × 5 × 5 cube?

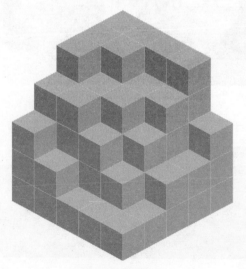

Answer on page 160

RIDDLE-ME-TEA: Discovering a fly in my tea, I asked the waiter if he could get me another cup, one without a fly. He came back with my new tea, I tasted it and guess what? The cheeky chancer had given me the same cup of tea back! But how did I know?

Answer on page 160

WHERE'S THE PAIR?: Only two of the shapes
below are exactly the same – can you find the matching pair?

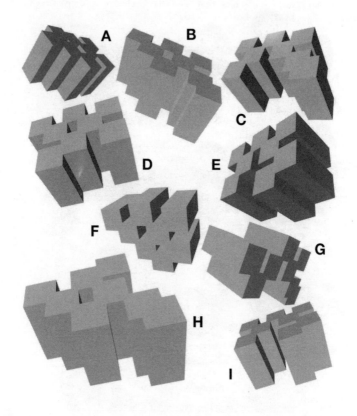

Answer on page 160

MIRROR IMAGE: Only one of these pictures is an exact mirror image of the first one? Can you spot it?

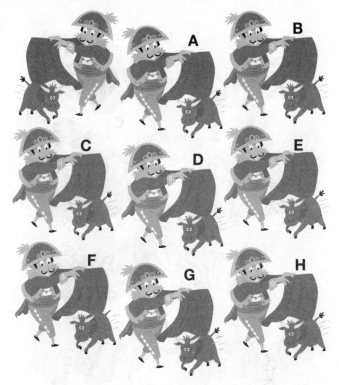

Answer on page 160

SUM TOTAL: Replace the question marks with mathematical symbols (+, −, × or ÷) to make a working sum.

$$10 \ ? \ 2 \ ? \ 4 \ ? \ 7 = 13$$

Answer on page 160

WHERE'S THE PAIR?: Only two of these
pictures are exactly the same. Can you spot the matching pair?

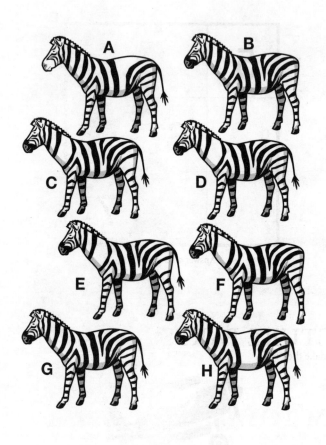

Answer on page 160

MAGIC SQUARES: Complete the square using nine

consecutive numbers, so that all rows, columns and large diagonals add up to the same total.

Answer on page 161

PICTURE PARTS: Which box has exactly the right

bits to make the pic?

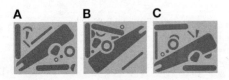

Answer on page 161

MAGIC SQUARES: Complete the square using nine

consecutive numbers, so that all rows, columns and large diagonals add up to the same total.

Answer on page 161

PICTURE PARTS: Which box has exactly the right

bits to make the pic?

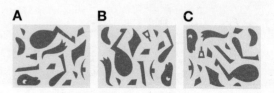

A **B** **C**

Answer on page 161

WHERE'S THE PAIR?: Only two of these
pictures are exactly the same – can you spot the matching pair?

Answer on page 161

BOX IT:

The value of each shape is the number of sides each shape has, multiplied by the number within it. Thus a square containing the number 4 has a value of 16. Find a block of four squares (two squares wide by two squares high) with a total value of exactly 50.

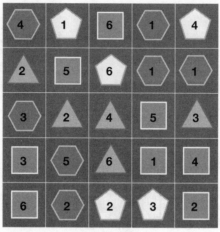

Answer on page 161

SUDOKU SIX:

Complete the first grid so that every row and column contain all the letters GLMRW and Y. Do the same with grid 2 and the numbers 12345 and 6. To decode the finished grid, add the numbers in the shaded squares to the letters in the matching squares in the second (ie: A + 3 = D, Y + 4 = C) to get six new letters which can be arranged to spell the name of a famous composer.

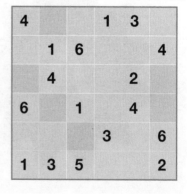

Answer on page 161

BOXES:
Playing the game of boxes, each player takes it in turns to join two adjacent dots with a line. If a player's line completes a box, the player wins the box and has another go. It's your turn in the game below. To avoid giving your opponent a lot of boxes, what's your best move?

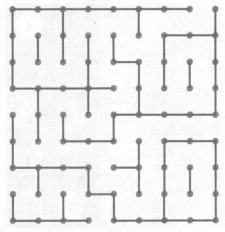

Answer on page 161

REVOLUTIONS:
Cog A has 12 teeth, cog B has 8 and cog C has 10. How many revolutions must cog A turn through to bring all three cogs back to these exact positions?

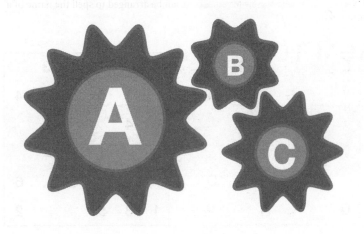

Answer on page 161

CHECKERS: Make a move for white so that eight black pieces are left, none of which are in the same column or row.

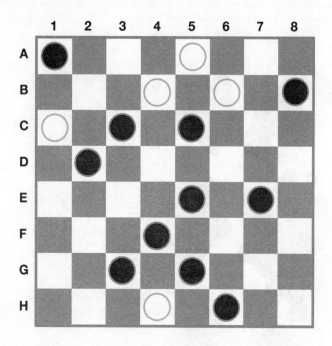

Answer on page 162

SUM TOTAL: Replace the question marks with mathematical symbols (+, −, ×, or ÷) to make a working sum.

Answer on page 162

WHERE'S THE PAIR?: Only two of the shapes
below are exactly the same – can you find the matching pair?

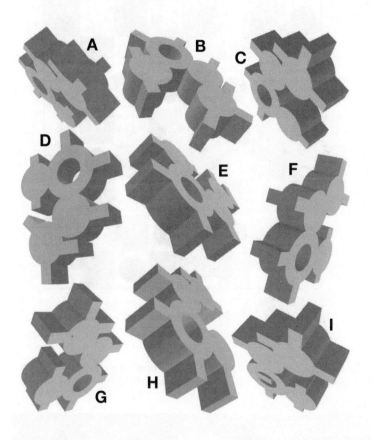

Answer on page 162

WHERE'S THE PAIR?: Only two of these

pictures are exactly the same. Can you spot the matching pair?

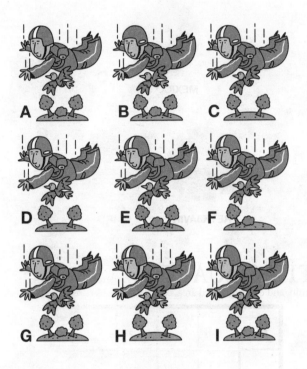

Answer on page 162

ODD CLOCKS: Cairo is 7 hours ahead of Mexico City, which is 5 hours behind Reykjavik. It is 10.30pm on Monday in Mexico City – What time is it in the other two cities?

MEXICO CITY

REYKJAVIK **CAIRO**

LATIN SQUARE: Complete the grid so that every row and column, and every outlined area, contains the letters A, B, C, D, E and F.

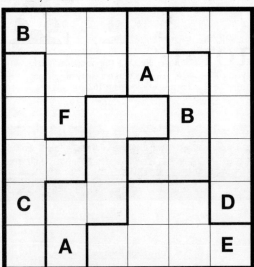

Answer on page 162

43

SAFECRACKER:
To open the safe, all the buttons must be pressed in the correct order before the "open" button is pressed. What is the first button pressed in your sequence?

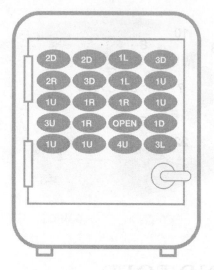

Answer on page 162

SUM TOTAL:
Replace the question marks with mathematical symbols (+, –, × or ÷) to make a working sum.

Answer on page 162

HUB SIGNS: What numbers should appear in the hubs of these number wheels?

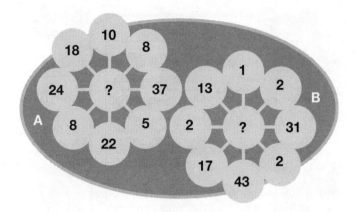

CUT AND FOLD: Which of the patterns below is created by this fold and cut?

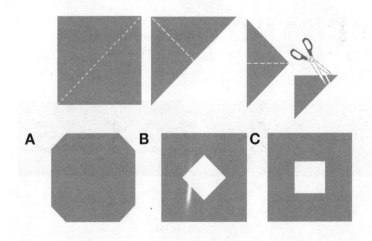

Answer on page 163

WHERE'S THE PAIR?: Only two of these
pictures are exactly the same. Can you spot the matching pair?

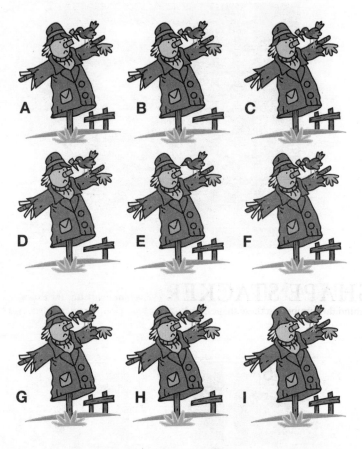

Answer on page 163

POTS OF DOTS: How many dots should there be in the hole in this pattern?

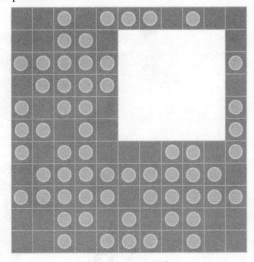

Answer on page 163

SHAPE STACKER: Can you work out the logic behind the numbers in these shapes, and suggest a number to replace the A and B?

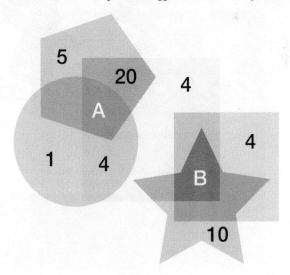

Answer on page 163

SUDOKU SIXPACK: Complete the grid so that
every row, column and long diagonal contains the numbers 1, 2, 3, 4, 5 and 6

2		4		5	6
		6		3	5
3			1		
					1
6	5				2
	2	1			

Answer on page 163

DOUBLE DRAT: All these shapes appear twice in the
box except one. Can you spot the singleton?

Answer on page 163

48

CUBISM: The shape below can be folded to make a cube. Which of the four cubes pictured below could it make?

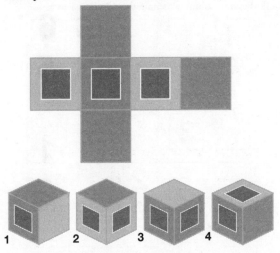

Answer on page 163

GAME OF TWO HALVES: Which two shapes below will pair up to create the top shape?

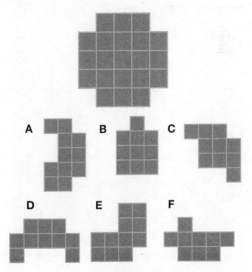

Answer on page 163

MORE OR LESS: The arrows indicate whether a

number in a box is greater or smaller than an adjacent number. Complete the
grid so that all rows and columns contain the numbers 1 to 5.

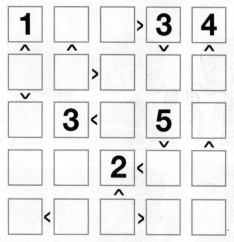

Answer on page 164

NUMBER SWEEP: The numbers in some squares

in the grid indicate the exact number of shaded squares that should surround
it. Colour in the squares until all the numbers are surrounded by the correct
number of shaded squares, and a number will be revealed!

	0		0		3			5		2	
0		0		3			8		5		0
	0		3		7			8		3	
0		3		6			8		5		0
	3		6		6	6		8		3	
3				3			8				
				4			8				
	8		6		6	7		8		6	
5		8		8			8		8		5
	5		5				8		6		
2		3		3			8		6		2
	0		0				5		2		

Answer on page 164

MIRROR IMAGE: Only one of these pictures is an
exact mirror image of the first one? Can you spot it?

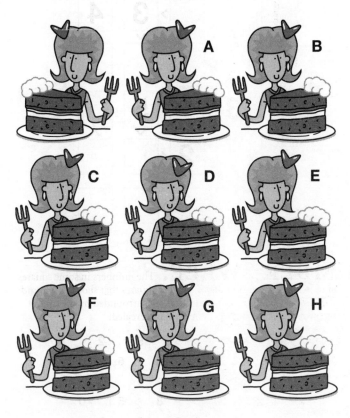

Answer on page 164

PAINT BY NUMBERS: Colour in the odd
numbers to reveal... What?

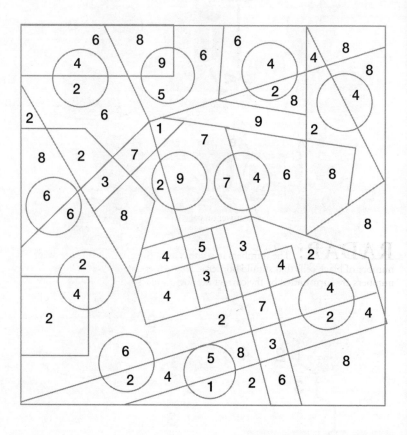

Answer on page 164

PICTURE PARTS: Which box contains exactly the right bits to make the pic?

Answer on page 164

RADAR: The numbers in some cells in the grid indicate the exact number of black cells that should border it. Shade these black, until all the numbers are surrounded by the correct number of black cells.

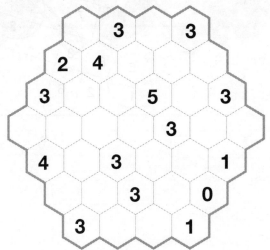

Answer on page 164

SILHOUETTE: Which of the coloured-in pics matches
our silhouette?

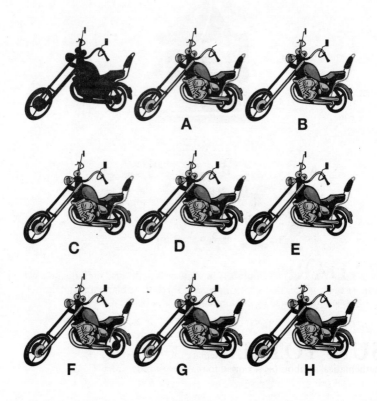

PICTURE PARTS: Which box has exactly the right bits to make the pic?

A   **B**   **C**

Answer on page 164

SUM TOTAL: Replace the question marks with mathematical symbols (+, -, x or ÷) to make a working sum.

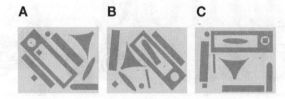

Answer on page 164

MEDIUM
PUZZLES

FOLLOW THAT: The sequence below follows a logical pattern. Can you work out what letter follows, and which way up it should be?

ABᗺAⱯⱯA?

Answer on page 164

FRACTION ACTION: Can you determine what fraction of this tiling job remains unfinished?

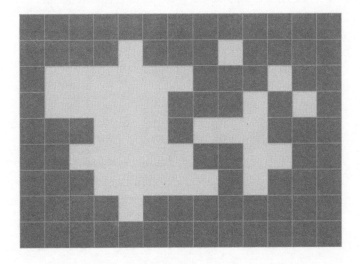

Answer on page 164

MASYU:
Draw a single continuous line around the grid that passes through all the circles. The line must enter and leave each box in the centre of one of its four sides.

Black Circle: Turn left or right in the box, and the line must pass straight through the next and previous boxes.

White Circle: Travel straight through the box, and the line must turn in the next and/or previous box.

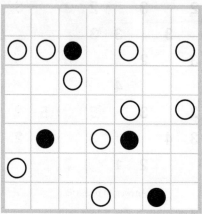

Answer on page 165

MATRIX:
Which of the boxed figures completes the set?

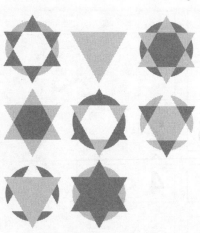
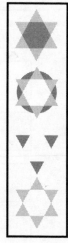

Answer on page 165

MINESWEEPER: The numbers in some squares in the grid indicate the exact number of black squares that should surround it. Shade these squares until all the numbers are surrounded by the correct number of black squares.

	2				2		1
2		3		2	3		3
	3		3	3			
3		2			6		5
			4				
2		3		5		5	2
3	4			3			2
		2	1		2		

Answer on page 165

MORE OR LESS: The arrows indicate whether a number in a box is greater or smaller than an adjacent number. Complete the grid so that all rows and columns contain the numbers 1 to 5.

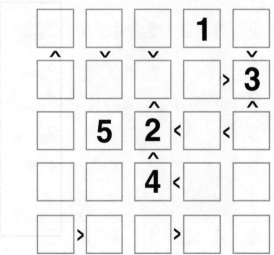

Answer on page 165

59

A PIECE OF PIE: Can you crack the pie code and work out what number belongs where the question mark is?

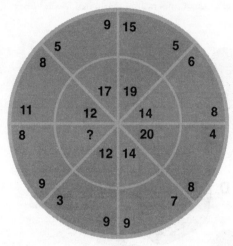

Answer on page 165

X AND O: The numbers around the edge of the grid describe the number of X's in the vertical, horizontal and diagonal lines connecting with that square. Complete the grid so that there is an X or O in every square.

2	3	2	2	4	3	3
4	O				X	3
2						4
3		X				2
3				X		4
3	X				X	3
3	4	3	1	4	5	2

Answer on page 165

WHERE'S THE PAIR?: Only two of these

pictures are exactly the same. Can you spot the matching pair?

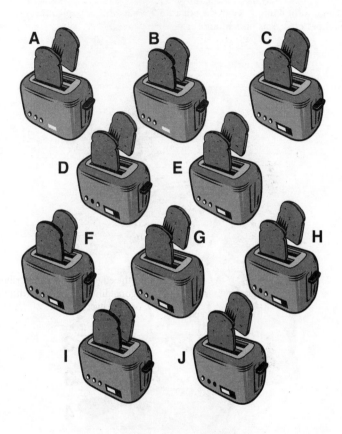

Answer on page 166

RIDDLE: Chef Gordon Ramsfoot was challenged one day to perfectly soft boil a goose egg, so that the white was all set and the yolk left perfectly runny. A goose egg, he discovers, takes exactly nine minutes to boil this way, but Gordon only has two egg timers – the old fashioned glass and sand type. One timer is for 4 minutes and the other for 7. Using the two timers, how can Gordon perfectly time his 9 minute egg?

Answer on page 166

SUM PEOPLE: Work out what number is represented by which person and replace the question mark.

Answer on page 166

SAFECRACKER:
To open the safe, all the buttons must be pressed in the correct order before the "open" button is pressed. What is the first button pressed in your sequence?

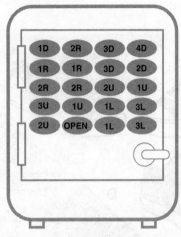

Answer on page 166

DICE PUZZLE:
What's the missing number?

Answer on page 166

MIRROR IMAGE: Only one of these pictures is an exact mirror image of the first one? Can you spot it?

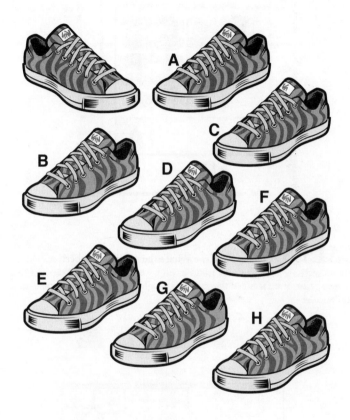

Answer on page 166

LATIN SQUARE:
Complete the grid so that every row and column, and every outlined area, contains the letters A, B, C, D, E and F.

Answer on page 166

SCALES:
The arms of these scales are divided into sections – a weight two sections away from the middle will be twice as heavy as a weight one section away. Can you arranged the supplied weights in such a way as to balance the whole scale?

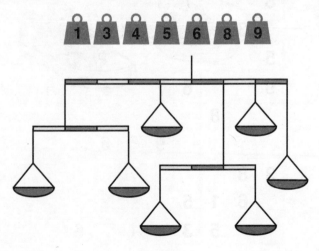

Answer on page 166

SIGNATURES: Can you crack the logical secret behind the numbers next to theses famous composers, and work out what number might be next to Mozart?

Beethoven 60

Tchaikovsky 72

Mozart ?

Schubert 36

Brahms 15

Answer on page167

SUDOKU: Complete the grid so that all rows and columns, and each outlined block of nine squares, contain the numbers 1, 2, 3, 4, 5, 6, 7, 8, and 9.

8			7	1		5		4
	3				2			7
5						1		
9			6	7		4		5
		8						
				9	5	6		
3	8				7			1
	6	1	5			2		
		5	3		1		6	

Answer on page 167

WHERE'S THE PAIR?: Only two of the shapes below are exactly the same – can you find the matching pair?

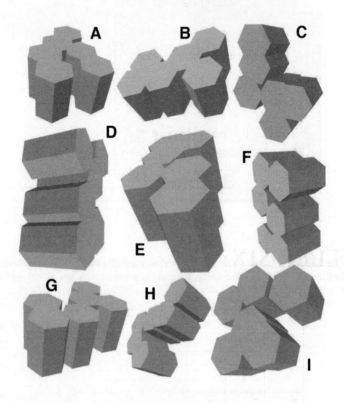

Answer on page 167

FLOOR FILLERS:
Below is a plan of a living room, showing fitted units that cannot be moved. Can you tile the whole floor using only the shape of tile shown? The tiles are not reversible!

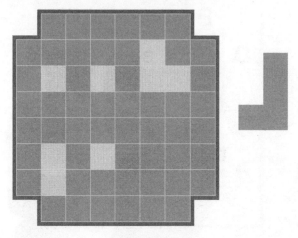

Answer on page 167

KILLER SIX:
Complete the grid so that all rows and columns contain the numbers 1, 2, 3, 4, 5 and 6. Areas with a dotted outline contain numbers that add up to the total shown.

9	6			11	
	1	12			15
9	7		1		
	12		11	9	
3		2			5
	13				

Answer on page 167

69

LATIN SQUARE: Complete the grid so that every row and column, and every outlined area, contains the letters A, B, C, D, E and F.

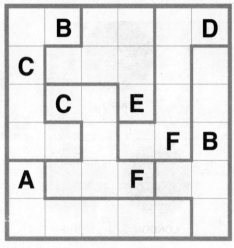

Answer on page 167

MASYU: Draw a single continuous line around the grid that passes through all the circles. The line must enter and leave each box in the centre of one of its four sides.

Black Circle: Turn left or right in the box, and the line must pass straight through the next and previous boxes.

White Circle: Travel straight through the box, and the line must turn in the next and/or previous box.

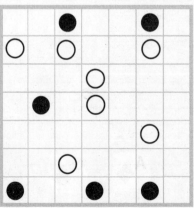

Answer on page 167

ODD CLOCKS: Sydney is 8 hours ahead of Cairo, which is 1 hour ahead of London. It is 8.20 pm on Saturday in Cairo – what time is it in the other two cities?

CAIRO

LONDON   **SYDNEY**

Answer on page 168

SHUFFLE: Fill up the shuffle box so that each row, column and long diagonal contains a Jack, Queen, King and Ace of each suit.

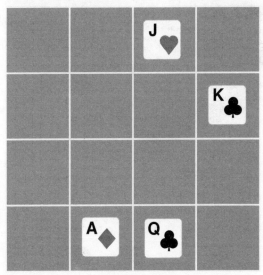

Answer on page 168

RIDDLE: Charlie is organizing his music collection. He manages to sort out a box of Jazz records and a box of Soul records before he has to rush off to give his nephew a guitar lesson. He puts the rest of the Jazz and Soul records into a third box. He quickly writes labels for all three boxes – Jazz, Soul and J&S. Unfortunately, in his haste, he puts the wrong labels on all three boxes. When he returns, how can he re-label his boxes correctly by listening to just one record?

Answer on page 168

SUDOKU:

Complete the grid so that all rows and columns, and each outlined block of nine squares, contain the numbers 1, 2, 3, 4, 5, 6, 7, 8 and 9.

8		9	6	1	4			3
	2				9	6	7	
5		3	7				4	
		6	9		7	4	8	5
4	3							
7			8		6	3		
9		1	2			8		6
6		7			3		2	
	5		4		8	7		1

Answer on page 168

SUM PEOPLE: Work out what number is represented by which person and fill in the question mark.

WHERE'S THE PAIR?: Only two of these
pictures are exactly the same. Can you spot the matching pair?

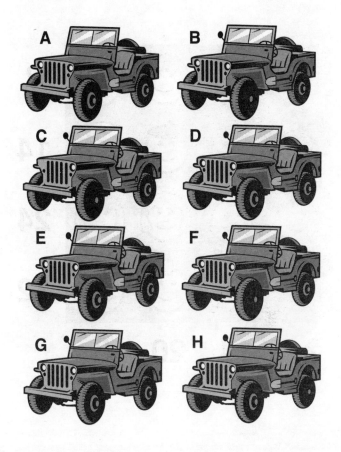

Answer on page 168

WHERE'S THE PAIR?: Only two of the shapes

below are exactly the same, can you find the matching pair?

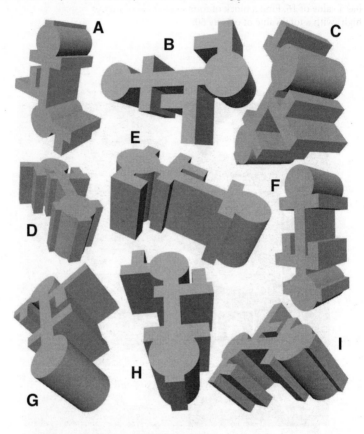

Answer on page 168

BOX IT: The value of each shape is the number of sides each shape has, multiplied by the number within it. Thus a square containing the number 4 has a value of 16. Find a block of four squares (two squares wide by two squares high) with a total value of exactly 60.

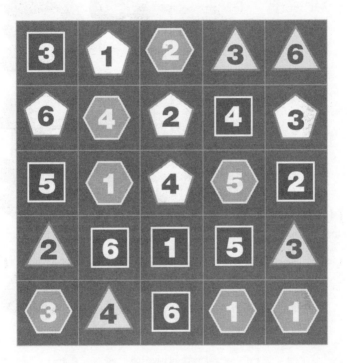

Answer on page 168

KILLER SIX:
Complete the grid so that all rows and columns contain the numbers 1, 2, 3, 4, 5 and 6. Areas with a dotted outline contain numbers that add up to the total shown.

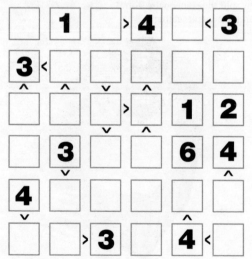

5	15	7	7
			2	18
11	1	8	
	6	7	
5		11	7	5
	9	2	

Answer on page 169

MORE OR LESS:
The arrows indicate whether a number in a box is greater or smaller than an adjacent number. Complete the grid so that all rows and columns contain the numbers 1 to 6.

Answer on page 169

SUDOKU: Couplet the grid so that all rows and columns, and each outlined block of nine squares, contain the numbers 1, 2, 3, 4, 5, 6, 7, 8 and 9.

9		4		6	8	5		3
1	3		9				8	
	6			4	5	1		2
		6	2	5		7	4	
	5				3			6
4	7			1		2		
	4	3		9	1			7
	8			3		4	6	9
7		2	6	8			5	1

Answer on page 169

THINK OF A NUMBER: Yellowbeard the
pirate had a treasure chest containing 720 gold coins following his latest raid. He took a third himself, his navigator and first mate took one eighth each and the rest of the crew split the rest equally. Tom the cabin boy got 20 coins, How many people were on the boat altogether?

Answer on page 169

MINI NONOGRAM: The numbers by each row
and column describe black squares and groups of black squares that are adjoining.
Colour in all the black squares and a six number combination will be revealed.

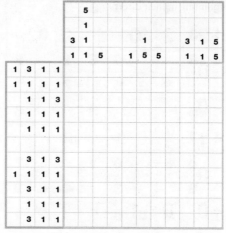

Answer on page 169

MORE OR LESS: The arrows indicate whether a
number in a box is greater or smaller than an adjacent number. Complete the
grid so that all rows and columns contain the numbers 1 to 6.

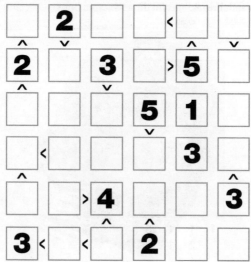

Answer on page 169

ARROWS: Complete the grid by drawing an arrow in each box that points in any one of the eight compass directions (N, E, S, W, NE, NW, SE, SW). The numbers in the outside boxes in the finished puzzle will reflect the number of arrows pointing in their direction.

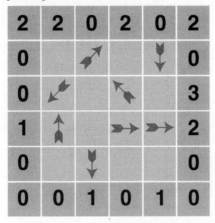

Answer on page 169

BATTLESHIPS: The numbers on the side and bottom of the grid indicate occupied squares or groups of consecutive occupied squares in each row or column. Can you finish the grid so that it contains three Cruisers, three Launches and three Buoys and the numbers tally?

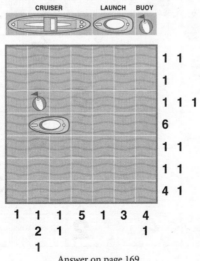

Answer on page 169

BOXES:
Playing the game of boxes, each player takes it in turns to join two adjacent dots with a line. If a player's line completes a box, the player wins the box and has another go. It's your turn in the game below. To avoid giving your opponent a lot of boxes, what's your best move?

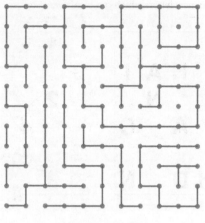

Answer on page 170

MORE OR LESS:
The arrows indicate whether a number in a box is greater or smaller than an adjacent number. Complete the grid so that all rows and columns contain the numbers 1 to 5.

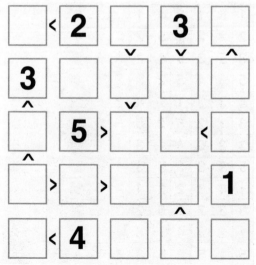

Answer on page 170

SUDOKU SIX:
Complete the first grid so that every row and column contains all the letters ACDHI and N. Do the same with grid 2 and the numbers 12345 and 6. To decode the finished grid, add the numbers in the yellow squares to the letters in the matching squares in the second (ie: A + 3 = D, Y + 4 = C) to get six new letters which can be arranged to spell the name of a city.

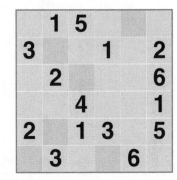

Answer on page 170

FIGURE IT OUT:
The sequence 12345 can be found once in the grid, reading up, down, backwards, forwards or diagonally. Can you pick it out?

1	5	1	2	4	1	2	5	2	1	2	3
2	2	2	1	5	2	2	2	4	2	3	2
3	5	3	5	4	2	3	3	3	3	1	1
5	3	4	5	2	3	3	2	4	4	2	3
4	3	3	1	3	4	4	1	2	2	5	2
3	1	2	5	2	5	5	3	5	3	4	3
3	2	3	4	1	3	4	4	4	3	4	5
5	2	3	3	5	3	4	5	3	3	3	5
1	4	3	2	2	4	2	3	5	2	2	1
3	3	7	1	5	2	3	5	2	5	1	3
1	2	3	4	3	5	4	4	4	1	3	2
5	1	5	2	5	3	5	3	4	3	2	1

Answer on page 170

LOOPLINK:
Connect adjacent dots with either horizontal or vertical lines to create a continuous unbroken loop which never crosses over itself. Some, but not all of the boxes are numbered. The numbers in these boxes tell you how many sides of that box are used by your unbroken line.

Answer on page170

SHAPE STACKER:
Can you work out the logic behind the numbers in these shapes, and the total of A x B x C?

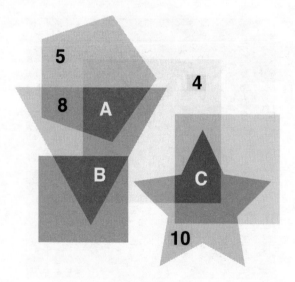

Answer on page 170

SILHOUETTE: Which of the coloured-in pics matches our silhouette?

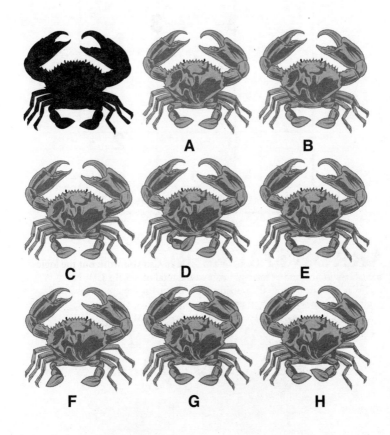

Answer on page 170

SUDOKU:
Complete the grid so that all rows and columns, and each outlined block of nine squares, contain the numbers 1, 2, 3, 4, 5, 6, 7, 8 and 9.

7							3	
1		4		2		5		9
8			9		6		7	
6	1		2	5				
		9						6
			6			9		
9	7			8		4		3
		5			1			7
2		6	4	9		8		1

Answer on page 171

ARROWS:
Complete the grid by drawing an arrow in each box that points in any one of the eight compass directions (N, E, S, W, NE, NW, SE, SW). The numbers in the outside boxes in the finished puzzle will reflect the number of arrows pointing in their direction.

Answer on page 171

BOXES:
Playing the game of boxes, each player takes it in turns to join two adjacent dots with a line. If a player's line completes a box, the player wins the box and has another go. It's your turn in the game below. To avoid giving your opponent a lot of boxes, what's your best move?

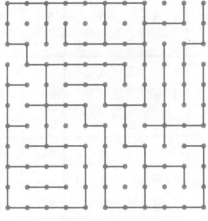

Answer on page 171

FIVE POINT PROBLEM:
Discover the pattern behind the numbers on these pentagons and fill in the blanks to complete the puzzle.

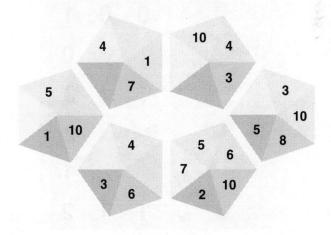

Answer on page 171

SAFECRACKER:
To open the safe, all the buttons must be pressed in the correct order before the "open" button is pressed. What is the first button pressed in your sequence?

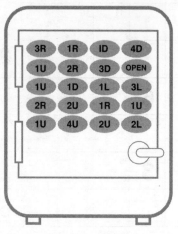

3R	1R	1D	4D
1U	2R	3D	OPEN
1U	1D	1L	3L
2R	2U	1R	1U
1U	4U	2U	2L

Answer on page 172

THE GREAT DIVIDE:
Divide the grid into four equal sized, equally shaped parts, each containing the numbers 1, 2, 3 and 4.

4			3
	1	1	3
	2	2	2	4
3	4	3	1	2
	4		1

Answer on page 172

KILLER SIX: Complete the grid so that all rows and columns contain the numbers 1, 2, 3, 4, 5 and 6. Areas with a dotted outline contain numbers that add up to the total shown.

3		11	10	14	
7					2
15	6			3	
	6		8	4	12
	3	5			
7			4		6

Answer on page 172

BEES AND BLOOMS: Every bloom ✿ has one bee 🐝 found horizontally or vertically adjacent to it. No bee can be in an adjacent square to another bee (even diagonally). The numbers by each row and column tell you how many bees are there. Can you locate all the bees?

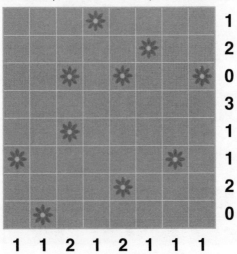

Answer on page 172

89

BOXES: Playing the game of boxes, each player takes it in turns to join two adjacent dots with a line. If a player's line completes a box, the player wins the box and has another go. It's your turn in the game below. To avoid giving your opponent a lot of boxes, what's your best move?

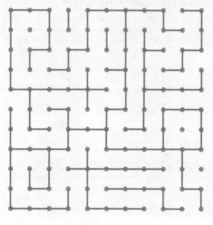

Answer on page 172

CHECKERS: Make a move for white so that eight black pieces are left, none of which are in the same column or row.

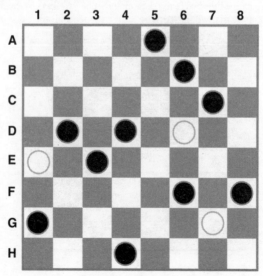

Answer on page 172

HIDDEN PARIS: The word PARIS can be found once
in the grid, reading up, down, backwards, forwards, or diagonally. Can you pick
it out?

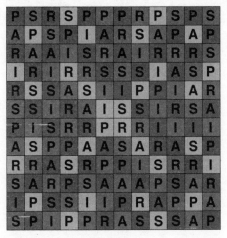

Answer on page 172

IN THE AREA: Can you work out the approximate area
that this crab is occupying?

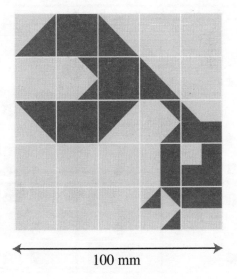

100 mm

Answer on page 172

X AND O:
The numbers around the edge of the grid describe the number of X's in the vertical, horizontal and diagonal lines connecting with that square. Complete the grid so that there is an X or O in every square.

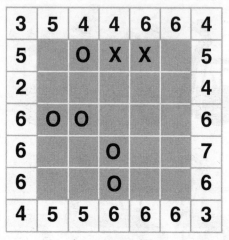

Answer on page 173

SUDOKU:
Complete the grid so that all rows and columns, and each outlined block of nine squares, contain the numbers 1, 2, 3, 4, 5, 6, 7, 8 and 9.

		1		3				4
			4	6			9	
2					5	7		
				2		3		5
1						8		
5	3			4			1	6
6		3	5		2			9
		8		9			5	
4				1			7	2

Answer on page 173

SILHOUETTE: Which of the coloured-in pics matches our silhouette?

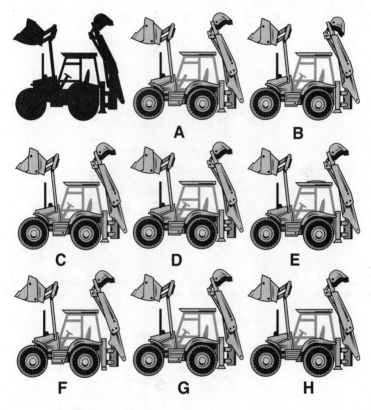

A B

C D E

F G H

Answer on page 173

93

RIDDLE: Geoff the farmer has to boat across the river with his dog, a chicken and a bag of grain. There is only room for Geoff and one passenger in the boat, and he can't leave the dog alone with the chicken, or the chicken alone with the grain... What can he do?

Answer on page 173

SHAPE STACKER:
Can you work out the logic behind the numbers in these shapes, and replace the question mark with a number?

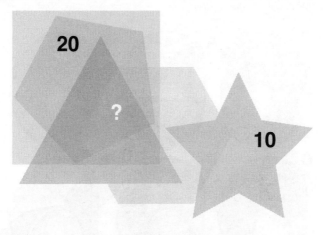

Answer on page 173

SIGNPOST:
Can you crack the logical secret behind the distances to these great cities, and work out how far it is to Melbourne?

Answer on page 173

MIRROR IMAGE: Only one of these pictures is an exact mirror image of the first one? Can you spot it?

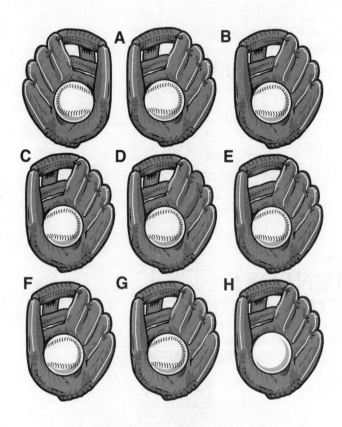

Answer on page 173

MASYU:
Draw a single continuous line around the grid that passes through all the circles. The line must enter and leave each box in the centre of one of its four sides.

Black Circle: Turn left or right in the box, and the line must pass straight through the next and previous boxes.

White Circle: Travel straight through the box, and the line must turn in the next and/or previous box.

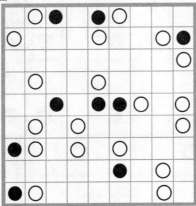

Answer on page 173

ODD CLOCKS:
Singapore is 12 hours ahead of Miami, which is 13 hours behind Tokyo. It is 11.05 pm on Wednesday in Miami – what time is it in the other two cities?

MIAMI

TOKYO   **SINGAPORE**

Answer on page 173

LATIN SQUARE: Complete the grid so that every row and column, and every outlined area, contains the letters A, B, C, D, E and F

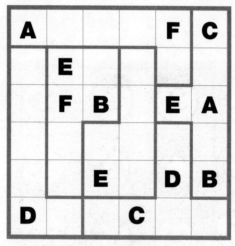

Answer on page 174

MAGIC SQUARES: Complete the square using nine consecutive numbers, so that all rows, columns and large diagonals add up to the same total.

Answer on page 174

SUM PEOPLE: Work out what number is represented by which person and replace the question mark.

Answer on page 174

99

SCALES:
The arms of these scales are divided into sections – a weight two sections away from the middle will be twice as heavy as a weight one section away. Can you arranged the supplied weights in such a way as to balance the whole scale?

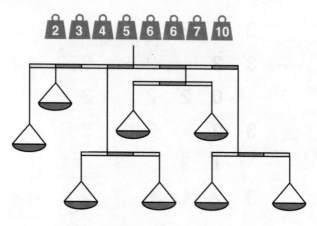

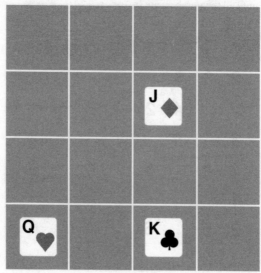

Answer on page 174

SHUFFLE:
Fill up the shuffle box so that each row, column and long diagonal contains a Jack, Queen, King and Ace of each suit.

Answer on page 174

LOOPLINK:
Connect adjacent dots with either horizontal or vertical lines to create a continuous unbroken loop which never crosses over itself. Some, but not all of the boxes are numbered. The numbers in these boxes tell you how many sides of that box are used by your unbroken line.

3	1	3	2	3	2
3	2		2	1	3
	0	2	2		3
3	2		2	2	2
	1	3		3	
3	2	1	1	3	2

Answer on page 174

MINESWEEPER:
The numbers in some squares in the grid indicate the exact number of black squares that should surround it. Shade these squares until all the numbers are surrounded by the correct number of black squares.

0	1		2	3			2
2	3	3		3		5	
		4	2	4	2	4	
3		4		2		3	2
2	4		5	4	4		3
1					4		
2	5		6	4	4		4
	3			2		3	

Answer on page 174

MINI NONOGRAM:
The numbers by each row and column describe black squares and groups of black squares that are adjoining. Colour in all the black squares and a six number combination will be revealed.

Column clues:

			1				1			
			1				1			1
	1	1	3		1	1	3			1
	3	1	1		3	1	1			1
	5	1	5		5	1	5		5	5	5

Row clues:

| 3 3 3 |
| 1 1 1 1 |
| 3 3 3 |
| 1 1 1 1 |
| 3 3 3 |
| |
| 3 3 1 |
| 1 1 1 1 1 |
| 1 1 1 1 1 |
| 1 1 1 1 1 |
| 3 3 1 |

Answer on page 175

SMALL LOGIC:
Three lucky ladies received flowers this morning. Using the clues below, can you work out who got which flowers, in which colour, and for what occasion?

1) The surprise flowers were roses, but not red ones.
2) Marianna received tulips, but it isn't her birthday.
3) Natasha's flowers were white, and she knew they would be.

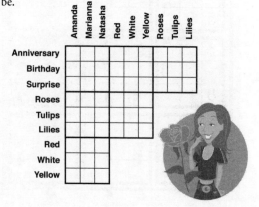

	Amanda	Marianna	Natasha	Red	White	Yellow	Roses	Tulips	Lilies
Anniversary									
Birthday									
Surprise									
Roses						
Tulips						
Lilies						
Red			
White			
Yellow			

Answer on page 175

FLOOR FILLERS: Below is a plan of the entrance pathway to a theatre, complete with spaces either side for plant pots. Below are some oddly shaped pieces of red carpet... Can you fill the floor with them?

Answer on page 175

SUDOKU: Fill in each row, column and 9x9 box with the numbers 1, 2, 3, 4, 5, 6, 7, 8, 9 once only.

4			1	3				8
					7			
5	9						4	
1			9	8				
				7		3		
8					1	6		
9			3					
			7		2			5
				4	5		2	

Answer on page 175

JIGSAW: Which four of the pieces below can complete the jigsaw and make a perfect square?

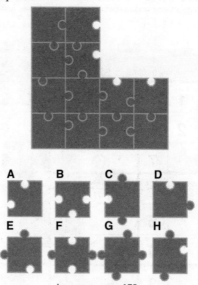

Answer on page 175

RADAR: The numbers in some cells in the grid indicate the exact number of black cells that should border it. Shade these black, until all the numbers are surrounded by the correct number of black cells.

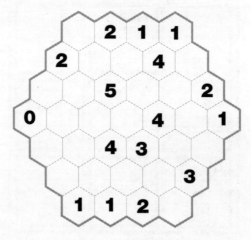

Answer on page 175

SUDOKU: Complete the grid so that all rows and columns, and each outlined block of nine squares, contain the numbers 1, 2, 3, 4, 5, 6, 7, 8, 9..

	1			3	6		2	9
9	2	8			7	3	6	
		7					4	8
	5		3		1	4		6
8		6		2	9	5	1	7
	7	4			8			3
5		3			2		7	
		2	7	8		9	5	1
	9		5		4			

Answer on page 176

HARD
PUZZLES

WHERE'S THE PAIR?: Only two of the
shapes below are exactly the same – can you find the matching pair?

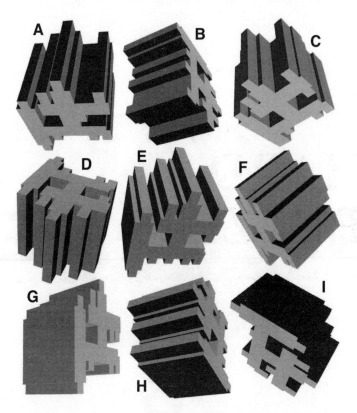

Answer on page 176

107

RIDDLE:

Pete goes back to visit the farm he lived on as a boy. From the town exit, he drives 3 miles east, then turns left and drives 4 miles north. Then he finds out there is a new road that leads directly from the town exit to the farm! How many miles would he have saved had he known that before?

Answer on page 176

MASYU:

Draw a single continuous line around the grid that passes through all the circles. The line must enter and leave each box in the centre of one of its four sides.

Black Circle: Turn left or right in the box, and the line must pass straight through the next and previous boxes.

White Circle: Travel straight through the box, and the line must turn in the next and/or previous box.

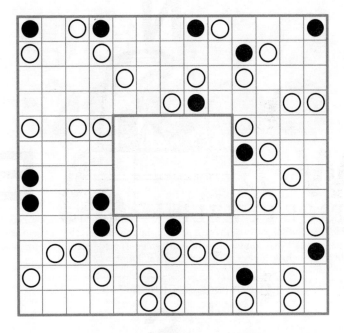

Answer on page 176

LOGIC SEQUENCE: The balls below have been

rearranged. Can you work out the new sequence of the balls from the clues given below?

There are two balls between the X and the triangle.
There are two balls between the star and the circle.
There is one ball between the star and the square.
The circle is immediately to the left of the X.

Answer on page 176

PRICE PUZZLE: At a swanky Bond Street jewellers, you

decide to spend some of your recent lottery win on some gifts for some of your closest friends. What combination of fourteen items made up of the four shown could you purchase for exactly a quarter of a million?

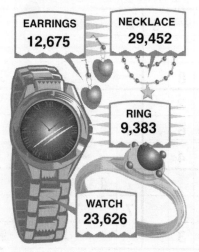

EARRINGS 12,675

NECKLACE 29,452

RING 9,383

WATCH 23,626

Answer on page 176

MINESWEEPER: The numbers in some squares in the
grid indicate the exact number of black squares that should surround it. Shade
these squares until all the numbers are surrounded by the correct number of
black squares.

3		2	1		2		
			2			3	1
3	3	1	2				0
	2			3		2	0
		1	1	3	2		1
	2	1		3		3	
2			3		4		3
	1	1		3		3	

Answer on page 176

MORE OR LESS SUDOKU: Complete
the grid so that all rows and columns, and each outlined block of nine squares,
contain the numbers 1, 2, 3, 4, 5, 6, 7, 8 and 9. The numbers in the arrowed squares
are bigger than the numbers in the squares the arrows are pointing at.

	9	2		6			
						7	
8				7	2		6
2							
6		4				5	
4							
	7		4	2		3	
		7			6		
3							9

Answer on page 176

NUMBER CHUNKS: Divide up the grid into four
equal size, equally shaped parts, each containing numbers that add up to 40.

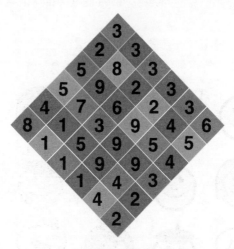

Answer on page 177

WHERE'S THE PAIR?: Only two of these
pictures are exactly the same. Can you spot the matching pair?

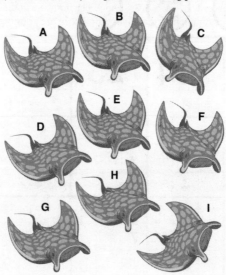

Answer on page 177

SUM PEOPLE: Work out what number is represented by which person and replace the question mark.

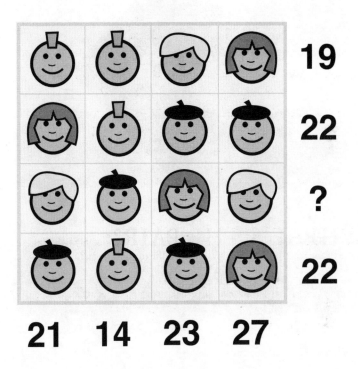

Answer on page 177

SILHOUETTE: Which of the coloured-in pics matches our silhouette?

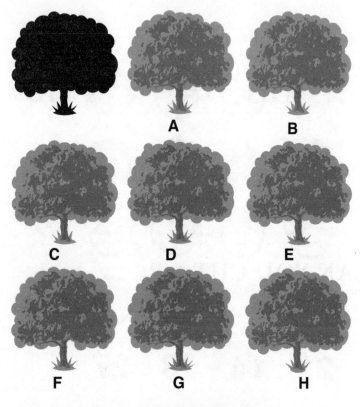

Answer on page 177

114

BITS AND PIECES: These ten pieces can be
arranged to spell out the name of a famous historical figure... but who?

Answer on page 177

CAN YOU CUT IT?: Cut two straight lines
through this shape to create three shapes that are identical.

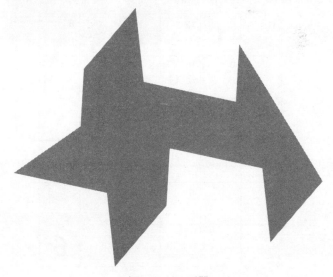

Answer on page 177

115

FIVE POINT PROBLEM: Discover the
pattern behind the numbers on these pentagons and fill in the blanks to complete
the puzzle.

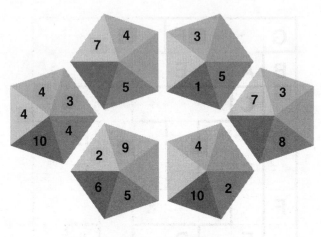

Answer on page 177

KILLER SIX: Complete the grid so that all rows and columns
contain the numbers 1, 2, 3, 4, 5 and 6. Areas with a dotted outline contain
numbers that add up to the total shown.

11	**1**	12			8
	9	10	3		
			10	8	
5	11			9	
		8	**5**		
5			5		**6**

Answer on page 177

LATIN SQUARE: Complete the grid so that every row

and column, and every outlined area, contains the letters A to H.

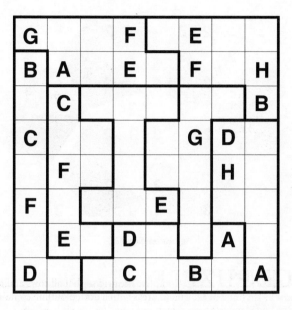

Answer on page 178

117

MINESWEEPER: The numbers in some squares in the grid indicate the exact number of black squares that should surround it. Shade these squares until all the numbers are surrounded by the correct number of black squares.

	2	3			2	1	1
2		3				2	
	2		4		3		
1		3		3		4	
	2		3	3	2	5	
1		4		1			
2			2		2		
	3		1	0		2	2

Answer on page 178

PRICE PUZZLE: Taking your wife, parents and kids to High Tea at a swish hotel in Bournemouth, you picked up the bill. The six of you had two cakes each and a big pot of tea cost you 4.95. The bill was exactly twenty pounds. How many eclairs did your family eat?

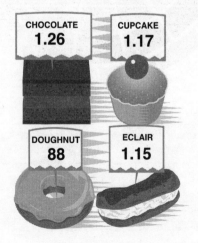

CHOCOLATE 1.26

CUPCAKE 1.17

DOUGHNUT 88

ECLAIR 1.15

Answer on page 178

ROULETTE:
The roulette ball is dropped into the wheel at the the 0 section. When the ball falls into a number 16 seconds later, it has travelled at an average speed of 3 metres per second clockwise, while the wheel has travelled at an average 2 metre per second in the other direction. The ball starts rolling 50 centimetres away from the wheel's centre. Where does it land? Take pi as having a value of exactly 3.2.

Answer on page 178

SHAPE STACKER: Can you work out the logic behind the numbers in these shapes, and the total of A × B × C?

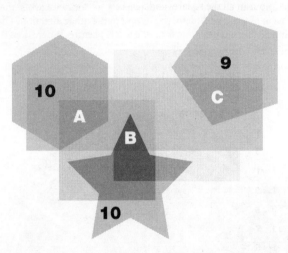

Answer on page 178

SUDOKU: Complete the grid so that all rows and columns, and each outlined block of nine squares, contain the numbers 1, 2, 3, 4, 5, 6, 7, 8 and 9.

	7				5		4	
			1		6			
2			3			1		8
		5				3		
			4	1				
3		9			7			6
7			8		4		3	
		2		9		5		
	5		6				8	1

Answer on page 178

MINI NONOGRAM: The numbers by each
row and column describe black squares and groups of black squares that are
adjoining. Colour in all the squares and a picture will be revealed.

				1	1		1	1									
				1	1		1	1				4		4			
				1	1		1	1		1		1		1		1	
			1	2	3	15	4	4	4	4	11	5	13	5	11	4	3
			1														
			3														
1	1	1	1														
		1	3														
		3	5														
1	1	1	7														
		1	5														
3	1	1	1														
1	1	1	5														
1	1	1	1														
		1	5														
			11														
			13														
			14														
			15														

Answer on page 179

SMALL LOGIC: After the bank robbery, Tex, Sixgun
and Hoss split up and headed for their hideouts. Can you name each bandit, the
horse he rode, and where he escaped to?

1) Hoss rode Blanco to a town
ending in the letter 'O'
2) Six-Gun MacGee didn't ride
Sunset, or to Dodge
3) Williams, who wasn't called Tex,
didn't ride to Reno

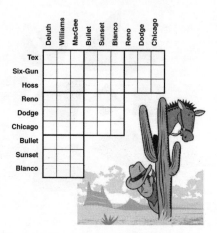

Answer on page 179

BATTLESHIPS: The numbers on the side and bottom of
the grid indicate occupied squares or groups of consecutive occupied squares in
each row or column. Can you finish the grid so that it contains four Cruisers, four
Launches and four Buoys and the numbers tally?

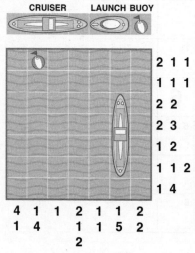

Answer on page 179

BITS AND PIECES: These pieces can be assembled
to spell the name of a city... Which?

Answer on page 179

KILLER SIX: Complete the grid so that all rows and columns
contain the numbers 1, 2, 3, 4, 5 and 6. Areas with a dotted outline contain
numbers that add up to the total shown.

3		6	7		11
11		8	3		
6			11	4	
6	12			3	
		3	6	8	
8				10	

Answer on page 179

CUBE VOLUME: These little cubes originally made a big cube measuring 12cm x 12cm x 12cm. Now some of the little cubes have been removed, can you work out what volume the remaining cubes have now? Assume all invisible cubes are present.

Answer on page 179

DICE PUZZLE: What's the missing number?

| 8 | 12 | 36 | ? |

Answer on page 179

KILLER SIX: Complete the grid so that all rows and columns contain the numbers 1, 2, 3, 4, 5 and 6. Areas with a dotted outline contain numbers that add up to the total shown.

15	6	9			7
		1	10		
		8	8	12	
4	10			6	
		9	**4**		
7				10	

Answer on page 180

MATRIX: Which of the four boxed figures completes the set?

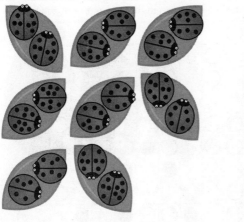

Answer on page 180

125

KILLER SUDOKU: Complete the grid so that all

rows and columns, and each outlined block of nine squares, contain the numbers
1, 2, 3, 4, 5, 6, 7, 8 and 9. Areas with a dotted outline contain numbers that add up
to the total shown.

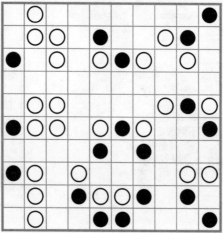

Answer on page 180

MASYU: Draw a single continuous line around the grid that passes

through all the circles. The line must enter and leave each box in the centre of
one of its four sides. Black Circle: Turn left or right in the box, and the line must
pass straight through the next and previous boxes. White Circle: Travel straight
through the box, and the line must turn in the next and/or previous box.

Answer on page 180

SUM PEOPLE: Work out which number is represented by which person and fill in the question mark

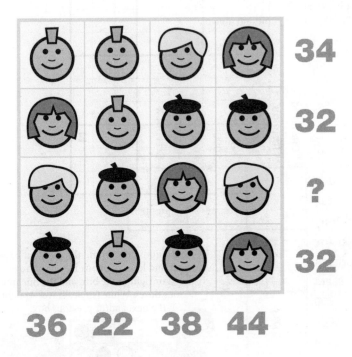

Answer on page 180

SMALL LOGIC: Jeff, Tony and Bill all won poker

tournaments in Las Vegas. Can you match up the first and last names with each player's poker nickname, and work out how much each player won?

1) Bill Sear's nickname isn't "Lucky".
2) Tony "The Diamond" isn't called Hopkins and won more than $500.
3) "Lucky" won a thousand dollars.

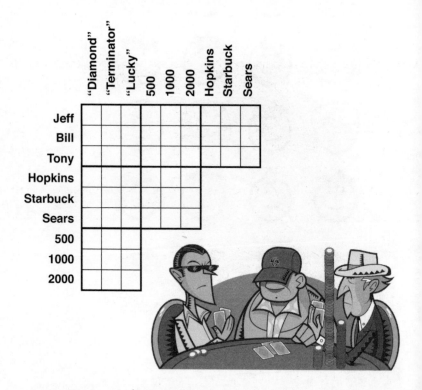

Answer on page 180

RIDDLE:

Your four greedy nieces are paying you a visit. You had saved a slice of pizza for lunch but when you open the fridge, you discover that one of the little darlings has already eaten it!

Katy says "Holly ate it!"
Holly says "Amy ate it!"
Amy says "Holly's lying!"
Poppy says "Well, it wasn't me!"
If just ONE of the girls' statements is true – who ate the pizza?

Answer on page 181

BITS AND PIECES: These pieces can be assembled
to spell the name of a giant of literature... Who?

Answer on page 181

CAN YOU CUT IT?: Turn this shape into three
shapes that are identical in size and shape by making one continuous cut.

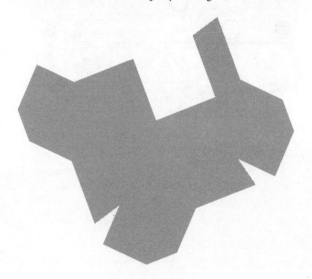

Answer on page 181

MASYU: Draw a single continuous line around the grid that passes through all the circles. The line must enter and leave each box in the centre of one of its four sides.

Black Circle: Turn left or right in the box, and the line must pass straight through the next and previous boxes.

White Circle: Travel straight through the box, and the line must turn in the next and/or previous box.

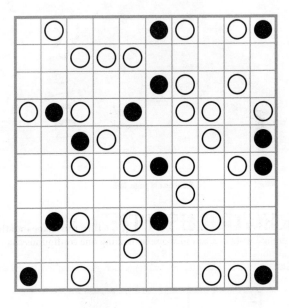

Answer on page 181

NUMBER MOUNTAIN: Replace the

question marks with numbers so that each pair of blocks adds up to the block directly above them.

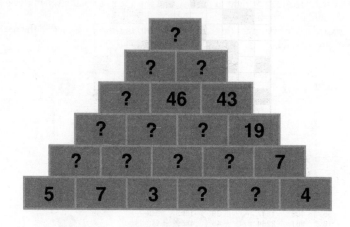

Answer on page 181

MORE OR LESS SUDOKU: Complete

the grid so that all rows and columns, and each outlined block of nine squares, contain the numbers 1, 2, 3, 4, 5, 6, 7, 8 and 9.

The numbers in the arrowed squares are bigger than the numbers in the squares the arrows are pointing at.

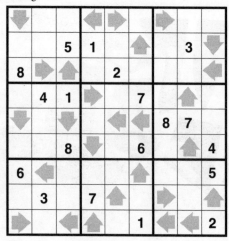

Answer on page 181

NUMBER FILL-IN: Find homes for all the listed
numbers to complete the grid.

51	354	4488		28	578	1990		82	9120	6780
96	225	7276		50	534	1095		25	8547	2450
99	560	4045		26	121	2725		62720		1114400
55	408	1547		39	1605	9676		35532		4967424
18	981	2264		45	4459	5442				

Answer on page 182

BITS AND PIECES: These pieces can be assembled
to spell the name of a famous painter... Who?

Answer on page 182

SMALL LOGIC: Three professors were each studying
different space phenomena, located in different directions and near different
planets. Can you work out exactly who was looking in which direction at what,
and what planet was near to each heavenly body?

1) Saturn was toward the West. Professor Green wasn't looking there.

2) The asteroid was near Jupiter. Fujyama wasn't looking at it.

3) Fujyama looked in the south, but not at a black hole.

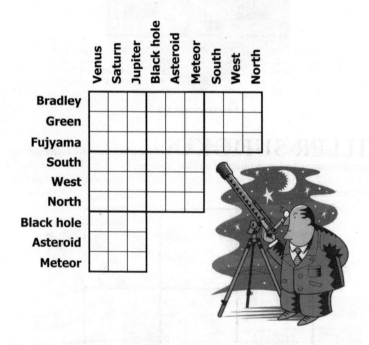

Answer on page 182

CUBE VOLUME: These little cubes originally made
a big cube measuring 18 cm x 18 cm x 18 cm. Now some of the little cubes have
been removed, can you work out what volume the remaining cubes have? Assume
all invisible cubes are present.

Answer on page 182

KILLER SUDOKU: Complete the grid so that all
rows and columns, and each outlined block of nine squares, contain the numbers
1, 2, 3, 4, 5, 6, 7, 8 and 9. Areas with a dotted outline contain numbers that add up
to the total shown.

7		16	9		12	9	16	
10			19					
10		**8**			25			
	16	5	6	14		5		23
5				15	13			
	19				11	10		
24	10	9	12			16		6
			14					
		5		8		**8**	10	

Answer on page 182

135

SMALL LOGIC: Phillipe, Luc and Bernard are

balloning in the mountains. From the clues below can you work out who travelled how far and landed in which country, and match each balloonist to their correct surname?

1) Phillipe travelled 50 miles, and he didn't land in Belgium.

2) Brunet (not Bernard), landed in Switzerland, more than 25 miles away from his take-off point.

3) The 25-mile flight landed in France, and wasn't piloted by Bernard or Dupont.

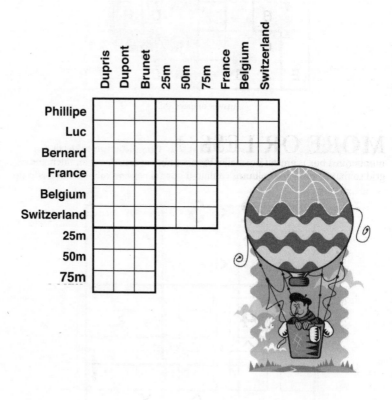

LATIN SQUARE: Complete the grid so that every row and column, and every outlined area, contains the letters A to H.

				F	G	D	
	H	G		E		C	F
F		A					
					E		
						A	
	B				D	H	
	C			H			
E	A	B		D	C		

Answer on page 182

MORE OR LESS: The arrows indicate whether a number in a box is greater or smaller than an adjacent number. Complete the grid so that all rows and columns contain the numbers 1 to 5.

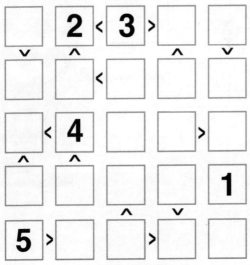

Answer on page 182

MINI NONOGRAM: The numbers by each
row and column describe black squares and groups of black squares that are
adjoining. Colour in all the black squares and a picture will be revealed.

				1					2								
				4		4	4	3	2	1							
				1	5	2	2	1	1	2	3	1	10	9	8		2
			1	1	4	1	1	5	1	1	2	11	1	1	1	12	2
1	4																
5	3																
4	2																
4	4																
3	1	5															
2	1	7															
1	9																
7																	
5																	
5																	
1	1	2	2														
5	1	1															
4	1	1															
1	1	2	2														
15																	

Answer on page 183

SCALES:
The arms of these scales are divided into sections – a weight two sections away from the middle will be twice as heavy as a weight one section away. Can you arranged the supplied weights in such a way as to balance the whole scale?

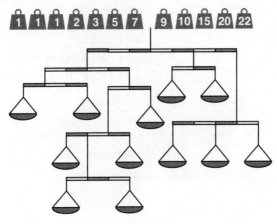

Answer on page 183

SHAPE STACKER:
Can you work out the logic behind the numbers in these shapes, and whether A divided by B = C, D or E?

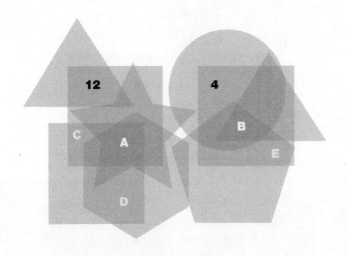

Answer on page 183

CAN YOU CUT IT?:
Turn this shape into three shapes that are identical in size and shape by making just two cuts.

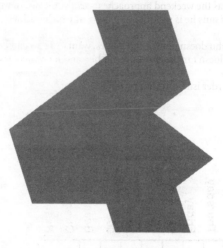

Answer on page 183

CUBISM:
The shape below can be folded to make a cube. Which of the four cubes pictured below could it make?

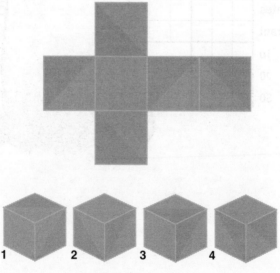

Answer on page 183

SMALL LOGIC:
Swordfish Beach coconuts are in great demand on Marlin Island for their size and sweetness. Palm-climber Ray has a bunch to collect as the weekend approaches – can you work out from the clues below how many nuts he is picking for whom, at which business, and when he must deliver?

1) Arthur, who doesn't make chocolates, wants 30 coconuts.
2) Big Dan doesn't make chocolates either, and he wants his coconuts on Saturday.
3) Friday's order isn't for Alice or the Beach Bar.

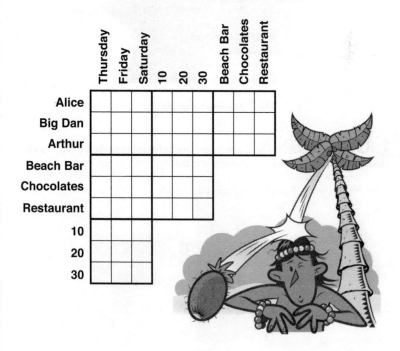

Answer on page 183

SCALES:
The arms of these scales are divided into sections – a weight two sections away from the middle will be twice as heavy as a weight one section away. Can you arranged the supplied the weights in such a way as to balance the whole scale?

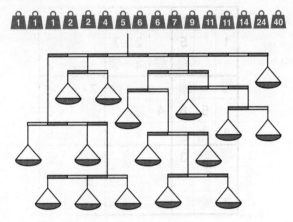

Answer on page 184

LOOPLINK:
Connect adjacent dots with either horizontal or vertical lines to create a continuous unbroken loop which never crosses over itself. Some (but not all) of the boxes contain numbers revealing exactly how many sides of that box are occupied by your unbroken line.

2		2	3		2		3
2	0	1		0	3	2	2
3		3	2		2	1	
2	0	2	1	2		2	2
	0		2	3		2	1
2	2		1		2		
		3	2		2	3	2
3	1		2	3	2		2

Answer on page 184

MORE OR LESS SUDOKU: Complete

the grid so that all rows and columns, and each outlined block of nine squares, contain the numbers 1, 2, 3, 4, 5, 6, 7, 8, and 9. The numbers in the arrowed squares are bigger than the numbers in the squares the arrows are pointing at.

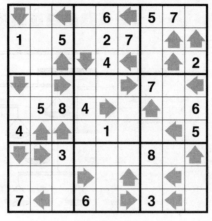

Answer on page 184

NUMBER MOUNTAIN: Replace the

question marks with numbers so that each pair of blocks adds up to the number on the block directly above them.

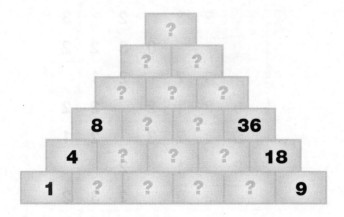

Answer on page 184

NUMBER CHUNKS: Divide up the grid into four
equal sized, equally shaped parts, each containing numbers that add up to 50.

8	9	8	7	6	4
9	3	6	1	5	7
7	1	9	4	7	3
9	2	9	5	6	3
2	1	2	9	9	3
5	5	5	5	9	7

Answer on page 184

SAFECRACKER: To open the safe, all the buttons must
be pressed in the correct order before the "open" button is pressed. What is the
first button pressed in your sequence?

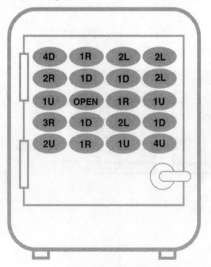

Answer on page 184

PRICE PUZZLE:
Buying the prizes for your local school fete, you have been given a budget of 100 pounds, which you managed to spend exactly. If you bought 6 bears and 18 items altogether, how many dolls did you buy?

Answer on page 184

CORNERED!:
Use the red corners to make the central number. What number should replace the question mark?

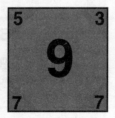

Answer on page 184

145

SYMMETRY: This picture, when finished, is symmetrical along a vertical line up the middle. Can you colour in the missing squares and work out what the picture is of?

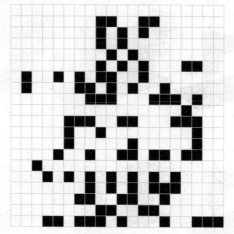

Answer on page 185

SUDOKU: Complete the grid so that all rows and columns, and each outlined block of nine squares, contain the numbers 1, 2, 3, 4, 5, 6, 7, 8 and 9.

			6				2	
	2					6		
8	9		4		3	1		7
	4	1				5		
						8		1
	7	8	5		6			
		2		4				5
1	3			5	2	9	8	6
9					1	3		

Answer on page 185

SILHOUETTE: Which of the coloured-in pics matches
our silhouette?

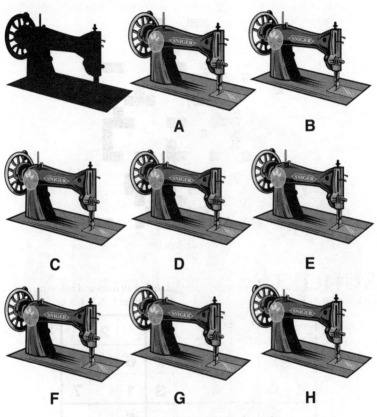

A

B

C

D

E

F

G

H

Answer on page 185

RIDDLE: Ten chocolate machines make truffles that weigh ten grams each. One day, one of the machines goes wrong and starts making truffles that only weigh 9.5 grams. If you weighed a truffle from each machine, you could find out which one has broken. But is there a way to find out which machine has gone wrong quicker than that?

Answer on page 185

MINI NONOGRAM: The numbers by each
row and column describe black squares and groups of black squares that are
adjoining. Colour in all the black squares and picture will be revealed.

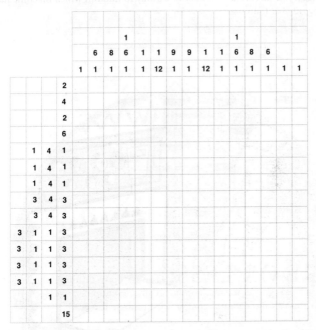

Answer on page 185

DICE PUZZLE: Which of these dice is not like the other three?

Answer on page 185

SCALES: The arms of these scales are divided into sections – a weight two sections away from the middle will be twice as heavy as a weight one section away. Can you arranged the supplied weights in such a way as to balance the whole scale?

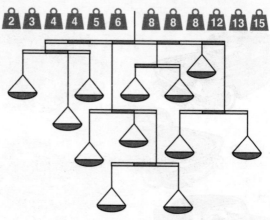

Answer on page 186

MORE OR LESS: The arrows indicate whether a number in a box is greater or smaller than an adjacent number. Complete the grid so that all rows and columns contain the numbers 1 to 6.

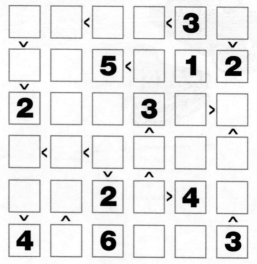

Answer on page 186

MIRROR IMAGE: Only one of these pictures is an exact mirror image of the first one. Can you spot it?

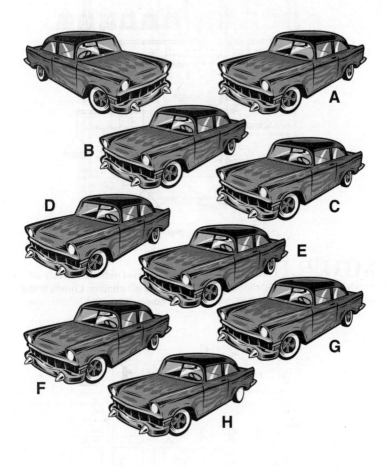

Answer on page 186

151

SUDOKU: Complete the grid so that the numbers 1, 2, 3, 4, 5, 6, 7, 8 and 9 appear once only in each column, row and 9x9 box.

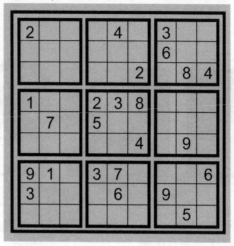

Answer on page 186

LOOPLINK: Connect adjacent dots with either horizontal or vertical lines to create a continuous unbroken loop which never crosses over itself. Some (but not all) of the boxes contain numbers revealing exactly how many sides of that box are occupied by your unbroken line.

2		2	0		2		2
3	0	3		3	0	1	3
3			1	3	2	3	2
	1	2	2		1		2
2				1		3	
2	2	3	2	2	3		1
		3		1		3	
2		2	2	2	3	2	2

Answer on page 186

CORNERED!: Use the red corners to make the central number the same way in all three cases. What number should replace the question mark?

Answer on page 186

REVOLUTIONS: Cog A has 16 teeth, cog B has 8, cog C has 9, cog D has 10 and cog E has 18. How many revolutions must cog A turn through to get all the cogs back into their original position?

Answer on page 186

ANSWERS

Page 7

MASYU

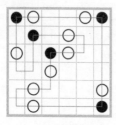

BIT AND PIECES
Answer: A and C, B and E,
H and F, D and G

Page 8

BOXES

Solution: A line on the top or
bottom of this square will only give
up one box to your opponent

CAN YOU CUT IT?

Page 9

SUDOKU

4	7	1	8	5	6	2	9	3
8	6	2	7	9	3	4	1	5
5	9	3	4	1	2	8	7	6
2	5	7	9	6	8	1	3	4
6	8	9	1	3	4	5	2	7
1	3	4	2	7	5	9	6	8
7	1	5	3	8	9	6	4	2
3	4	6	5	2	1	7	8	9
9	2	8	6	4	7	3	5	1

Page 10

WHERE'S THE PAIR?
Answer: C and E are the pair

Page 11

RIDDLE
Answer: It was driven there in winter,
when the lake was frozen.

Page 12

ODD CLOCKS
Answer: 3.35 am on Wednesday in
London; 11.35 pm on Tuesday in
Buenos Aires

SUM TOTAL
Solution: $22 + 8 \div 5 - 3 = 3$

Page 13

CHECKERS

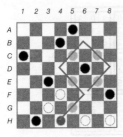

CUT AND FOLD
Answer: A

Page 14

DOUBLE DRAT

GAME OF TWO HALVES
Solution: C and D

Page 15

GRIDLOCK
Answer: B. Each row and column in the grid contains four dark and three light squares, and numbers that total 10

MASYU

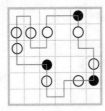

Page 16

MINI NONOGRAM

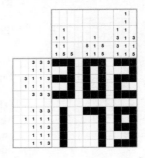

PICTURE PARTS
Answer: A

Page 17

MIRROR IMAGE
Answer: G

Page 18

WHERE'S THE PAIR?
Answer: B and E are the pair

Page 19

SUM PEOPLE
Solution: 23

 2

 4

 6

 9

Page 20

SUDOKU

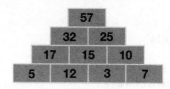

Page 21

SHAPE SHIFTING

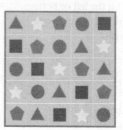

NUMBER MOUNTAIN

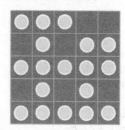

Page 22

POTS OF DOTS

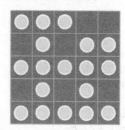

BOCK PARTY
Answer: 37

Page 23

BOXES
Solution: A line on the left or bottom of this square will only give up one box to our opponent

Page 24

CATS AND COGS
Answer: Down

CUT AND FOLD
Answer: A

Page 25

RIDDLE
Answer: 20 times. 9, 19, 29, 39, 49, 59, 69, 79, 89, 90, 91, 92, 93, 94, 95, 96, 97, 98 and twice in 99.

SUM TOTAL
Solution: $8 \times 3 \div 6 \times 2 = 8$

Page 26

ODD CLOCKS
Answer: 5.05 am on Friday in Tokyo
1.05 am on Friday in Karachi

POTS OF DOTS
Solution: 19

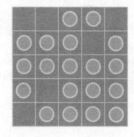

Page 27

RIDDLE
Answer: Because nobody knew it was World War One at the time

Page 28

GAME OF TWO HALVES
Solution: B and F

MATRIX
Solution: Each horizontal and vertical line contains one dog with a white ear.
Each line contains two dogs with a white patched eye.
Each line contains two dogs with their tongues out.
The missing image must have a white patched eye, no white ear, and the tongue out.

Page 29

WHERE'S THE PAIR?
Answer: D and H are the pair

Page 30

BITS AND PIECES
Answer: A, C, G and H, B, D, E and F
(The letters are A and B)

BLOCK PARTY
Answer: 42

Page 31

RIDDLE-ME-TEA
Answer: I had put sugar in my tea, and the "new" cup, which should have been unsugared, was sweet!

Page 32

WHERE'S THE PAIR?
Answer: E and I are the pair

Page 33

MIRROR IMAGE
Answer: G

SUM TOTAL
Solution: $10 \div 2 \times 4 - 7 = 13$

Page 34

WHERE'S THE PAIR?
Answer: C and E are the pair.

Page 35

MAGIC SQUARES

5	10	3
4	6	8
9	2	7

PICTURE PARTS
Answer: B

Page 36

MAGIC SQUARE

8	13	6
7	9	11
12	5	10

PICTURE PARTS
Answer: B

Page 37

WHERE'S THE PAIR?
Answer: C and G are the pair

Page 38

BOX IT

SUDOKU SIX
Solution: MOZART

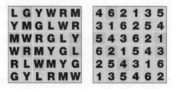

Page 39

BOXES
Solution: A line on the left or right of this square will only give up one box to your opponent

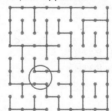

REVOLUTIONS
Answer: 10 revolutions of cog A, which will make exactly 15 revolutions of cog B and 12 revolutions of cog C

Page 40

CHECKERS

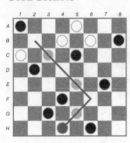

SUM TOTAL
Answer:
A) 6 – Add opposite numbers and multiply the integers of the total
B) 12 – Multiply the opposite numbers, then multiply the integers of the total

Page 41

WHERE'S THE PAIR?
Answer: A and G are the pair

Page 42

WHERE'S THE PAIR?
Answer: E and I are the pair

Page 43

ODD CLOCKS
Answer: 3.30 am on Tuesday in Reykjavic. 5.30 am on Tuesday in Cairo

LATIN SQUARE

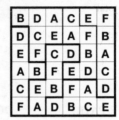

Page 44

SAFECRACKER

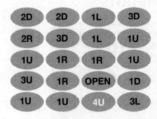

SUM TOTAL
Solution: $14 \times 2 \div 7 + 1 = 5$

Page 45

HUB SIGNS
Answer:
A) 6 – Add opposite numbers and multiply the integers of the total
B) 12 – Multiply the opposite numbers, then multiply the integers of the total

CUT AND FOLD
Answer : B

Page 46

WHERE'S THE PAIR?
Answer: B and H are the pair

Page 47

POTS OF DOTS

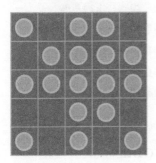

SHAPE STACKER
Answer: A = 20 and B = 160
The numbers represent the number of sides in the shape they occupy. When shapes overlap, the numbers are multiplied. 5 x 4 x 1 = 20 and 4 x 4 x 10 = 160

Page 48

SUDOKU SIXPACK

2	1	4	3	5	6
1	4	6	2	3	5
3	6	5	1	2	4
5	3	2	6	4	1
6	5	3	4	1	2
4	2	1	5	6	3

DOUBLE DRAT

Page 49

CUBISM
Answer: 4

GAME OF TWO HALVES
Solution: C and E

163

Page 50

MORE OR LESS

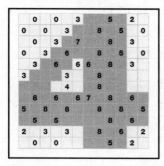

NUMBER SWEEP

Page 51

MIRROR IMAGE
Answer: G

Page 52

PAINT BY NUMBERS
Solution: A Footballer

Page 53

PICTURE PARTS
Answer: C

RADAR

Page 54

SILHOUETTE
Answer: D

Page 55

PICTURE PARTS
Answer: C

SUM TOTAL
Solution: $35 - 7 \div 4 - 4 = 3$

Page 57

FOLLOW THAT
Answer: B, the right way up. Two letters the same are followed by a letter the right way up. Two letters the same way up are followed by a B

FRACTION ACTION
Answer: There are 117 tiles in the finished job, 36 of which are missing. 117 divided by 9 is 13, and 36 divided by 9 is 4. So 4/13ths of the job remains unfinished

Page 58

MASYU

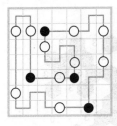

MATRIX

Solution: Each vertical and horizontal line contains one light shaded, one dark shaded and one plain white circle. Each line also contains one light shaded, one dark shaded and one plain white hexagon. Each line contains right-side-up triangles in light shading, dark shading and plain white. Finally each line contains two inverted triangles in light shading and one in dark shading. The missing image should be of a plain white circle with a white hexagon and both triangles in light shading

Page 59

MINESWEEPER

MORE OR LESS

2	4	3	1	5
5	2	1	4 > 3
1	5	2 < 3 < 4
3	1	4 < 5	2
4 > 3	5 > 2	1

Page 60

A PIECE OF PIE

Answer: 16. The inner numbers are made up of the two outer numbers of the previous segment of the same colour. 9 + 7= 16

X AND O

2	3	2	2	4	3	3
4	O	O	O	O	X	3
2	X	O	O	X	O	4
3	O	X	O	X	O	2
3	O	O	X	X	O	4
3	X	O	O	O	X	3
3	4	3	1	4	5	2

ANSWERS

Page 61

WHERE'S THE PAIR?
Answer: D and H are the pair

Page 62

RIDDLE
Answer: Gordon puts his egg in the water and starts both his timers at once. When the 4 minute timer is done, he flips it (4 minutes gone). When the 7 minute timer is done he flips it (7 minutes gone). At this point there is one minute to go on the 4 minute timer. When the 4 minute timer finishes (8 minutes gone) Gordon flips the 7 once more to let the 1 minute it has run go back the other way. 9 minutes.

Page 63

SUM PEOPLE
Solution: 22

3
4
5
8

Page 64

SAFECRACKER

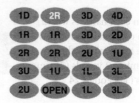

DICE PUZZLE
Answer: F

Page 65

MIRROR IMAGE
Answer: E

Page 66

LATIN SQUARE

B	A	E	D	C	F
F	E	A	C	D	B
E	B	D	A	F	C
D	F	C	E	B	A
C	D	F	B	A	E
A	C	B	F	E	D

SCALES

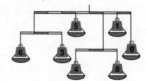

166

Page 67

SIGNATURES
Answer: 24
Each vowel in each name is worth
1 point, each consonant is worth 3.
Multiply one total by the other to
make the number. 2 vowels (2) times
4 consonants (12) equals 24

SUDOKU

8	2	9	7	1	6	5	3	4
1	3	6	4	5	2	8	9	7
5	4	7	9	3	8	1	2	6
9	1	2	6	7	3	4	8	5
6	5	8	1	2	4	3	7	9
4	7	3	8	9	5	6	1	2
3	8	4	2	6	7	9	5	1
7	6	1	5	8	9	2	4	3
2	9	5	3	4	1	7	6	8

Page 68

WHERE'S THE PAIR?
Answer: B and D are the pair.

Page 69

FLOOR FILLERS

KILLER SIX

4	3	1	2	6	5
5	1	6	4	2	3
3	2	5	1	4	6
6	4	3	5	1	2
1	5	2	6	3	4
2	6	4	3	5	1

Page 70

LATIN SQUARE

F	B	C	A	E	D
C	D	F	B	A	E
D	C	A	E	B	F
E	A	D	C	F	B
A	E	B	F	D	C
B	F	E	D	C	A

MASYU

Page 71

ODD CLOCKS
Answer: 7.20 pm on Saturday in London.

SHUFFLE

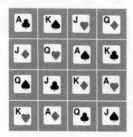

Page 72

RIDDLE
Answer: This is possible only if all the boxes are incorrectly labelled. Charlie takes one record from the box labelled J&S. If it's a Jazz record, then the (wrongly labelled) box it came from must be Jazz. If the (wrongly labelled) box marked Soul isn't Jazz, it can only be J&S. If he had taken out a Soul record then the box it came from must be Soul and the box marked Jazz must be J&S.

Page 73

SUDOKU

8	7	9	6	1	4	2	5	3
1	2	4	3	5	9	6	7	8
5	6	3	7	8	2	1	4	9
2	1	6	9	3	7	4	8	5
4	3	8	5	2	1	9	6	7
7	9	5	8	4	6	3	1	2
9	4	1	2	7	5	8	3	6
6	8	7	1	9	3	5	2	4
3	5	2	4	6	8	7	9	1

Page 74

SUM PEOPLE
Solution: 16

Page 75

WHERE'S THE PAIR?
Answer: B and F are the pair

Page 76

WHERE'S THE PAIR?
Answer: B and G are the pair

Page 77

BOX IT

Page 78

KILLER SIX

1	6	4	3	5	2
4	5	3	1	2	6
5	1	2	6	4	3
6	2	1	4	3	5
2	3	6	5	1	4
3	4	5	2	6	1

MORE OR LESS

6	1	5 >	4	2 <	3
3 <	4	6	2	5	1
5	6	4 >	3	1	2
1	3	2	5	6	4
4	2	1	6	3	5
2	5 >	3	1	4 <	6

Page 79

SUDOKU

9	2	4	1	6	8	5	7	3
1	3	5	9	2	7	6	8	4
8	6	7	3	4	5	1	9	2
3	1	6	2	5	9	7	4	8
2	5	8	4	7	3	9	1	6
4	7	9	8	1	6	2	3	5
6	4	3	5	9	1	9	2	7
5	8	1	7	3	2	4	6	9
7	9	2	6	8	4	3	5	1

THINK OF A NUMBER

Answer: 18. Yellowbeard got 240, the navigator and best mate got 180 between them leaving 300. If Tom got 20, there must be 15 crew

Page 80

MINI NONOGRAM

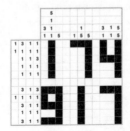

MORE OR LESS

1	2	6	3 <	4	5
2	1	3	6 >	5	4
4	3	2	5	1	6
5 <	6	1	4	3	2
6	5 >	4	1	2	3
3 <	4 <	5	2	6	1

Page 81

ARROWS

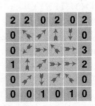

BATTLESHIPS

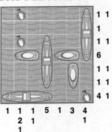

Page 82

BOXES
Solution: A line on the left or right of this square will only give up one box to your opponent

MORE OR LESS

1 < 2	5	3	4
3	1	4	2	5
4	5 > 3	1 < 2
5 > 3 > 2	4	1
2 < 4	1	5	3

Page 83

SUDOKU SIX
$A+1 = B$, $C+2 = E$, $N+4 = R$, $I+3 = L$, $D+5 = I$, $H+6 = N$
Answer: BERLIN

FIGURE IT OUT

1	5	1	2	4	1	2	5	2	1	2	3
2	2	2	1	5	2	2	2	4	2	3	2
3	5	3	5	4	2	3	3	3	3	1	1
5	3	4	5	2	3	3	2	4	4	2	3
4	3	3	1	3	4	4	1	2	2	5	2
3	1	2	5	2	5	5	3	5	3	4	3
3	2	3	4	1	3	4	4	4	3	4	5
5	2	3	3	5	3	4	5	3	3	3	5
1	4	3	2	2	4	2	3	5	2	2	1
3	3	7	1	5	2	3	5	2	5	1	3
1	2	3	4	3	5	4	4	4	1	3	2
5	1	5	2	5	3	5	3	4	3	2	1

Page 84

LOOPLINK

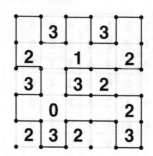

SHAPE STACKER
Answer: 2376
The numbers represent the number of sides in the shape they occupy. When shapes overlap, the numbers are added. A: $3+4+5 = 12$
B: $4+4+3 = 11$,
C: $10+4+4 = 18$
$12 \times 11 \times 18 = 2376$

Page 85

SILHOUETTE
Answer: E

Page 86

SUDOKU

7	9	2	8	1	5	6	3	4
1	6	4	7	2	3	5	8	9
8	5	3	9	4	6	1	7	2
6	1	7	2	5	9	3	4	8
5	4	9	1	3	8	7	2	6
3	2	8	6	7	4	9	1	5
9	7	1	5	8	2	4	6	3
4	8	5	3	6	1	2	9	7
2	3	6	4	9	7	8	5	1

ARROWS

Page 87

BOXES

Solution: A line on the top or right of this square wil only give up one box to your opponent

FIVE POINT PROBLEM

Solution: Each pentagon contains numbers that add up to 30, with the sides facing each other on adjoining pentagons showing the numbers 1 to 12 clockwise

ANSWERS

Page 88

SAFECRACKER

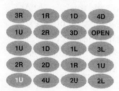

THE GREAT DIVIDE

4				3
	1		1	3
	2	2		2	4
3	4	3		1	2
	4			1

Page 89

KILLER SIX

1	2	6	4	3	5
3	4	5	1	6	2
4	6	3	5	2	1
5	1	2	6	4	3
6	3	1	2	5	4
2	5	4	3	1	6

BEES AND BLOOMS

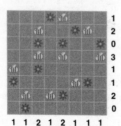

Page 90

BOXES

Solution: A line on the top or bottom of this square will only give up one box to your opponent

CHECKERS

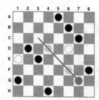

Page 91

HIDDEN PARIS

IN THE AREA

Answer: 3500 square millimetres. Each 20 x 20 square represents 400 mm². 3 squares, 5 half-square triangles, 4 half-squares, 1 quarter square and 8 8th of a square triangles are used

172

Page 92

X AND O

3	5	4	4	6	6	4
5	O	O	X	X	X	5
2	X	O	O	O	O	4
6	O	O	X	X	X	6
6	X	X	O	X	X	7
6	X	X	O	X	X	6
4	5	5	6	6	6	3

SUDOKU

9	8	1	2	3	7	5	6	4
3	7	5	4	6	1	2	9	8
2	4	6	9	8	5	7	3	1
8	6	7	1	2	9	3	4	5
1	9	4	3	5	6	8	2	7
5	3	2	7	4	8	9	1	6
6	1	3	5	7	2	4	8	9
7	2	8	6	9	4	1	5	3
4	5	9	8	1	3	6	7	2

Page 93

SILHOUETTE
Answer: G

Page 94

RIDDLE
Answer: Geoff can take the chicken over and come back for the dog; then take the dog over, swap it for the chicken on the other side and come back for the grain. He leaves the chicken and takes the grain over, leaving it with the dog and finally returning for the chicken

Page 95

SHAPE STACKER
Answer: 360.
The numbers represent the number of sides in the shape they occupy. Where shapes overlap, the numbers are multiplied 3 x 4 x 5 x 6 = 360

SIGNPOST
Answer: 117
Take the alphabetical position of the first letter of the city, and multiply by the number of letters in the word 13 (M) × 9 = 117

Page 96

MIRROR IMAGE
Answer: F

Page 97

MASYU

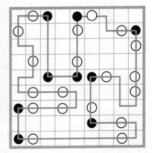

ODD CLOCKS
Answer: 12.05 pm on Thursday in Tokyo;
11.05 am Thursday in Singapore

Page 98

LATIN SQUARE

A	B	D	E	F	C
B	E	A	F	C	D
C	F	B	D	E	A
E	D	C	B	A	F
F	C	E	A	D	B
D	A	F	C	B	E

MAGIC SQUARES

6	5	10
11	7	3
4	9	8

Page 99

SUM PEOPLE
Solution: 23

 2

 4

 6

 9

Page 100

SCALES

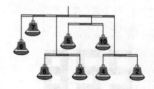

SHUFFLE

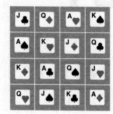

Page 101

LOOPLINK

3	1	3	2	3	2
3	2		2	1	3
	0	2	2		3
3	2		2	2	2
	1	3		3	
3	2	1	1	3	2

MINESWEEPER

Page 102

MINI NONOGRAM

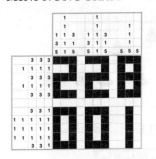

SMALL LOGIC

Page 103

FLOOR FILLERS

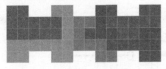

SUDOKU

4	7	2	1	3	9	5	6	8
3	8	6	4	5	7	2	1	9
5	9	1	2	6	8	7	4	3
1	6	7	9	8	3	4	5	2
2	5	9	6	7	4	3	8	1
8	3	4	5	2	1	6	9	7
9	2	5	3	1	6	8	7	4
6	4	8	7	9	2	1	3	5
7	1	3	8	4	5	9	2	6

Page 104

JIGSAW
Answer: A, C, G, and H

RADAR

Page 105

SUDOKU

4	1	5	8	3	6	7	2	9
9	2	8	1	4	7	3	6	5
3	6	7	2	9	5	1	4	8
2	5	9	3	7	1	4	8	6
8	3	6	4	2	9	5	1	7
1	7	4	6	5	8	2	9	3
5	8	3	9	1	2	6	7	4
6	4	2	7	8	3	9	5	1
7	9	1	5	6	4	8	3	2

Page 107

WHERE'S THE PAIR?
Answer: B and H are the pair

Page 108

RIDDLE
Answer: 2 miles. Pythagoras tells us the square of the hypotenuse on a right-angled triangle is equal to the sum of the squares of the other two sides. Pete's trip east and north are the two sides, so the sum of the squares is $3 \times 3 + 4 \times 4$, or 25. The direct route is therefore 5 miles (the square root of 25). His journey was 7 miles, so he would have saved 2

Page 109

MASYU

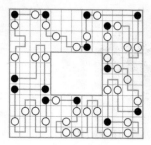

Page 110

LOGIC SEQUENCE

PRICE PUZZLE
Answer: 5 rings, 4 necklaces, 3 pairs of earrings and 2 watches 46,915 + 117,808 + 38,025 + 47,252 = 250,000

Page 111

MINESWEEPER

MORE OR LESS SUDOKU

1	7	9	2	8	6	5	4	3
2	5	6	9	3	4	8	7	1
4	8	3	1	5	7	2	9	6
7	2	5	3	6	9	4	1	8
9	6	8	4	2	1	3	5	7
3	4	1	5	7	8	9	6	2
6	9	7	8	4	2	1	3	5
5	1	2	7	9	3	6	8	4
8	3	4	6	1	5	7	2	9

Page 112

NUMBER CHUNKS

WHERE'S THE PAIR?
Answer: B and G are the pair

Page 113

SUM PEOPLE
Solution: 22

 3

4

 5

9

Page 114

SILHOUETTE
Answer: B

Page 115

BITS AND PIECES

CAN YOU CUT IT?

Page 116

FIVE POINT PROBLEM

Solution: Starting at the bottom right each pentagon contains numbers that add up to 25, and sides facing each other on adjoining pentagons add 2

KILLER SIX

5	1	2	4	6	3
6	3	4	1	2	5
4	2	6	3	5	1
3	5	1	6	4	2
2	6	3	5	1	4
1	4	5	2	3	6

Page 117

LATIN SQUARE

G	B	H	F	A	E	C	D
B	A	D	E	C	F	G	H
A	C	F	G	D	H	E	B
C	H	A	B	F	G	D	E
E	F	G	A	B	D	H	C
F	D	C	H	E	A	B	G
H	E	B	D	G	C	A	F
D	G	E	C	H	B	F	A

Page 118

MINESWEEPER

PRICE PUZZLE

Answer: 20 – 4.95 (for
the pot of tea) = 15.05
5 doughnuts (4.40) 4 cupcakes
(4.68) 2 chocolate cakes (2.52) and
three eclairs (3.45) make up the
rest of the bill

Page 119

ROULETTE

Answer: In the 0 space.
The ball travels at a speed of 5
metres per second (relative to the
wheel) for 16 seconds, making
a distance of 8000 centimetres
in a clockwise direction. The
circumference of the wheel is 320
(well, 319.96!) centimetres (2 x pi
(3.14) x radius (50.95 cm)). The
ball must then travel exactly 25
laps of the wheel (8000 divided by
320 = 25), placing it back in the 0
space where it started.

Page 120

SHAPE STACKER

Answer: 4004.
The numbers represent the number of
sides in the shape they occupy. When
shapes overlap, the numbers are added
together
A: 6 + 4 + 4 = 14   B: 10 + 4 + 4 + 4
= 22   C: 5 + 4 + 4 = 13
14 x 22 x 13 = 4004

SUDOKU

1	7	3	2	8	5	6	4	9
5	9	8	1	4	6	2	7	3
2	4	6	3	7	9	1	5	8
4	1	5	9	6	8	3	2	7
6	2	7	4	1	3	8	9	5
3	8	9	5	2	7	4	1	6
7	6	1	8	5	4	9	3	2
8	3	2	7	9	1	5	6	4
9	5	4	6	3	2	7	8	1

Page 121

MINI NONOGRAM

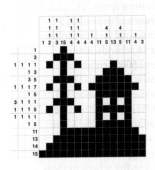

Page 122

SMALL LOGIC

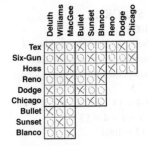

BATTLESHIPS

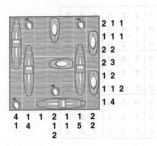

Page 123

BITS AND PIECES

KILLER SIX

2	1	6	3	4	5
4	3	5	1	2	6
6	4	3	5	1	2
5	2	4	6	3	1
1	6	2	4	5	3
3	5	1	2	6	4

Page 124

CUBE VOLUME

Answer: 1232 cubic centimetres. Each little cube measures 2 x 2 x 2 cm, or 8 cubic centimetres, and there are 154 little cubes left. 8 x 154 = 1232

DICE PUZZLE

Answer: 27. Add the top and side faces, then multiply by the front face

Page 125

KILLER SIX

6	1	4	2	3	5
5	3	1	6	4	2
4	2	6	3	5	1
3	4	2	5	1	6
1	6	5	4	2	3
2	5	3	1	6	4

MATRIX

Solution: Each vertical and horizontal line contains one leaf pointing top left and two pointing top right. Each vertical and horizontal line contains two images where the ladybirds are facing in different directions and one where they are facing the same way. Each vertical and horizontal line contains a total of 45 spots on all ladybirds

Page 126

KILLER SUDOKU

MASYU

Page 127

SUM PEOPLE

5

11

7

13

Page 128

SMALL LOGIC

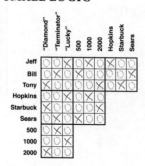

Page 129

RIDDLE

Answer: Poppy. If Katy or Holly's statements are true, then Poppy's must also be true. If Poppy is telling the truth, we can't tell who ate the pizza. So Amy is telling the truth, and Poppy ate it.

Page 130

BITS AND PIECES

Miguel de Cervantes

CAN YOU CUT IT?

Page 131

MASYU

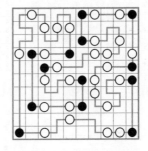

Page 132

NUMBER MOUNTAIN

```
            179
         90    89
      44    46    43
   22    22    24    19
 12    10    12    12    7
5    7    3    9    3    4
```

MORE OR LESS SUDOKU

7	1	3	6	9	5	4	2	8
4	2	5	1	7	8	6	3	9
8	9	6	4	2	3	1	5	7
2	4	1	9	8	7	5	6	3
5	6	9	2	3	4	8	7	1
3	7	8	5	1	6	2	9	4
6	8	2	3	4	9	7	1	5
1	3	4	7	5	2	9	8	6
9	5	7	8	6	1	3	4	2

ANSWERS

Page 133

NUMBER FILL-IN

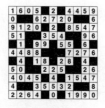

BITS AND PIECES

August Renoir

Page 134

SMALL LOGIC

Page 135

CUBE VOLUME

Answer: 4347 cubic centimetres. Each little cube measures 3 x 3 x 3 cm, or 27 cubic centimetres, and there are 161 little cubes left.

161 x 27 = 4347

KILLER SUDOKU

5	2	9	1	6	8	3	4	7
1	3	7	9	2	4	6	8	5
4	6	8	7	3	5	1	9	2
6	7	1	4	5	9	2	3	8
3	9	4	2	8	1	5	7	6
2	8	5	6	7	3	4	1	9
7	1	6	8	4	2	9	5	3
8	4	3	5	9	6	7	2	1
9	5	2	3	1	7	8	6	4

Page 136

SMALL LOGIC

Page 137

LATIN SQUARE

B	E	C	A	F	G	D	H
D	H	G	B	E	A	C	F
F	D	A	C	B	H	G	E
G	F	H	D	A	E	B	C
H	G	E	F	C	B	A	D
C	B	F	E	G	D	H	A
A	C	D	G	H	F	E	B
E	A	B	H	D	C	F	G

MORE OR LESS

4	2 < 3 > 1	5
1	3 < 5	2	4
2 < 4	1	5 > 3
3	5	2	4	1
5 > 1	4 > 3	2

Page 138

MINI NONOGRAM

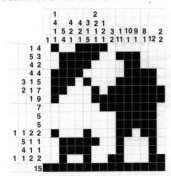

Page 139

SCALES

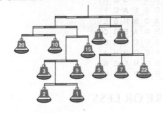

SHAPE STACKER

Answer: C
Count the sides on each shape.
Where shapes overlap their values are
multiplied together.
(A) 4 x 4 x 6 x 10 = 960
(B) 1 x 3 x 4 x 5 = 60
960 divided by 60 = 16, as does C

Page 140

CAN YOU CUT IT?

CUBISM
Answer: 4

Page 141

SMALL
LOGIC

	Thursday	Friday	Saturday	10	20	30	Beach Bar	Chocolates	Restaurant
Alice	X	O	O	O	X	O	O	X	O
Big Dan	O	X	X	O	O	X	O	O	X
Arthur	X	O	O	O	X	O	O	O	X
Beach Bar	O	X	X	O	O	X			
Chocolates	X	O	O	O	X	O			
Restaurant	O	O	O	O	O	X			
10	O	O	X						
20	X	O	O						
30	O	X	O						

183

ANSWERS

Page 142

SCALES

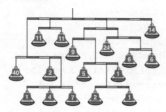

LOOPLINK

2		2	3		2			3
2	0	1		0	3	2	2	
		3	2			2	1	
3	0	2	1	2		2		2
2	0		2	3		2	1	
	2		1		2			
2		3	2		2	3	2	
	1		2	3	2			2

Page143

MORE OR LESS SUDOKU

9	2	4	1	6	8	5	7	3
1	3	5	9	2	7	6	8	4
8	6	7	3	4	5	1	9	2
3	1	6	2	5	9	7	4	8
2	5	8	4	7	3	9	1	6
4	7	9	8	1	6	2	3	5
6	4	3	5	9	1	8	2	7
5	8	1	7	3	2	4	6	9
7	9	2	6	8	4	3	5	1

NUMBER MOUNTAIN

Page 144

NUMBER CHUNKS

8	9	8	7	6	4
9	3	6	1	5	7
7	1	9	4	7	3
9	2	9	5	6	3
2	1	2	9	9	3
5	5	5	5	9	7

SAFECRACKER

Page 145

PRICE PUZZLE
Answer: Also six.
6 bears (29.28) + 2 cars (24.94) + 4
trains (23.88) +
6 dolls (21.90) = £100

CORNERED!
Answer: 68. Add the left hand red
corners together and subtract the
total from that of the right hand
corners multiplied together.
3 + 1 = 4. 8 x 9 = 72. 72 – 4 = 68

Page 146

SYMMETRY

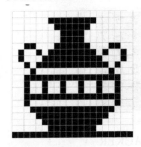

SUDOKU

7	1	3	6	9	5	4	2	8
4	2	5	1	7	8	6	3	9
8	9	6	4	2	3	1	5	7
2	4	1	9	8	7	5	6	3
5	6	9	2	3	4	8	7	1
3	7	8	5	1	6	2	9	4
6	8	2	3	4	9	7	1	5
1	3	4	7	5	2	9	8	6
9	5	7	8	6	1	3	4	2

Page 147

SILHOUETTE
Answer: F

Page 148

RIDDLE
Answer: In the 9 space.
The ball travels at a speed of 5 metres per second (relative to the wheel) for 20 seconds, making a distance of 10,000cm clockwise. The circumference of the wheel is 320 (well, 319.96!) centimetres (2 x pi (3.14) x radius (50.95 cm)). The ball must then travel exactly 31.25 laps of the wheel (10,000 divided by 320 = 31.25), placing it one quarter of the way around the wheel in a clockwise direction, in the 9 space.

Page 149

MINI MONOGRAM

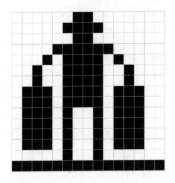

DICE PUZZLE
Answer: D. The right hand 2 should be turned 90 degrees

Page 150

SCALES

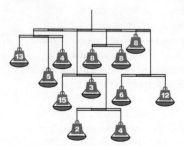

MORE OR LESS

```
5  1 < 4  2 < 3  6
3  4  5 < 6  1  2
2  6  1  3  5 > 4
1 < 2 < 3  4  6  5
6  3  2  5 > 4  1
4  5  6  1  2  3
```

Page 151

MIRROR IMAGE
Answer: C

Page 152

SUDOKU

2	8	9	6	4	7	3	1	5
4	5	7	1	8	3	6	2	9
6	3	1	9	5	2	7	8	4
1	9	4	2	3	8	5	6	7
8	7	2	5	9	6	4	3	1
5	6	3	7	1	4	8	9	2
9	1	8	3	7	5	2	4	6
3	2	4	4	6	1	9	7	8
7	4	6	8	2	9	1	5	3

LOOPLINK

```
2     2  0     2     2
3  0  3     3  0  1  3
3        1  3  2  3  2
   1  2  2     1     2
2           1     3
2  2  3  2  2  3     1
      3     1     3
2     2  2  2  3  2  2
```

Page 153

CORNERED!
Answer: 32. Using opposite red corners, subtract the smaller number from the larger. Then multiply the two totals together:
9 – 1 = 8, 7 – 3 = 4, 4 x 8 = 32

REVOLUTIONS
Answer: 45 revolutions of cog A. This will in turn make exactly 90 revolutions of cog B, 80 revolutions of cog C, 72 revolutions of cog D and 40 revolutions of cog E

YOUR PUZZLE NOTES